LEIGH LINLEY

GREAT

YORKSHIRE

BEER

GOOD BEER • GOOD FOOD
GOOD PEOPLE

GREAT NORTHERN

Great Northern Books

PO Box 213, Ilkley, LS29 9WS

www.greatnorthernbooks.co.uk

Every effort has been made to acknowledge correctly and contact the copyright holders of material in this book. Great Northern Books apologises for any unintentional errors or omissions, which should be notified to the publisher.

ISBN: 978-0-9572951-5-5

Design and layout: David Burrill

Printed in India

CIP Data

A catalogue for this book is available from the British Library

THE SUN IS SET WITHIN A MOUTH
OF BLACKENED STEEL & FLAME,
AS FIRE DRAWS THE CHARACTER
FROM EVERY SINGLE GRAIN.

A STORY TOLD A THOUSAND TIMES
IN EVERY DROP OF ALE,
FROM FIELD THROUGH FLAME & SETTING SUN,
TO MIDNIGHT BEST & PALE.

About the author

Leigh Linley has been writing about beer and food since 2007 on his popular blog, *The Good Stuff*. His work has also been published in *Beer Magazine*, *Culture Vulture*, *Leeds Guide* and has worked with Marketing Leeds promoting the pubs of Leeds.

He lives in Leeds with his wife, Louise, and his infamous Border terrier, Wilson.

Contents

Foreword

Yorkshire beer. Those two words have long been natural partners. Some of the most famous names in British brewing are from Yorkshire. Some of them are still with us.

Perhaps ten or so years ago, despite of course having some classic bitters and fantastic independent family brewers, Yorkshire had perhaps fallen behind some other parts of the country when it came to the new wave of British brewing. In many areas, new exciting microbreweries were starting up, brewing many styles of beer, some traditional, many not. There was a sense perhaps, with some notable exceptions, of Yorkshire resting on past laurels.

Well not any more. Yorkshire is now home to 123 breweries, making it by some way the nation's leading county for beer. This is not just a championship winning performance, but a trend, with 19 new breweries opening in the last year alone.

Now it has to be said, you certainly won't find Yorkshire beer fans failing to boast about this table topping accolade, nor should we, but what is even more important and pleasing is that this is very much about quality as well as quantity.

Yorkshire's new breweries and beers are now as diverse as Yorkshire itself. Great beer is being brewed all over the three ridings; from the great cities to the national parks; from the far north (Swaledale) to the deepest south (southern Sheffield); from the disputed west (Saddleworth) to the far east (the Yorkshire Coast). There are flavours that build on classic Yorkshire bitter and British styles, many look much further afield for inspiration and hops; all brewed by a generation of passionate, talented craft brewers who are committed to using the best quality ingredients.

This vibrancy and diversity, this thrill to the senses, especially the palate, is reflected in Leigh Linley's *Great Yorkshire Beer*. A very timely and equally attractive journey around some of

the groundbreaking, award-winning breweries that have done so much to give us a thrilling present and a great future for the great Yorkshire pint.

With great knowledge, obvious passion and an appropriate sense of Yorkshire pride, Leigh takes us round to meet the men and women who are making Yorkshire top of the national chart, as well as giving us great recipes matched with some of the county's top new brews.

Of course, as the Chair of the Parliamentary Save the Pub Group, I must state that the place to enjoy this great produce is in the many and different pubs of Yorkshire. One of the many great joys of touring England's most beautiful county from north to south, from east to west, is to sample this great local beer, in good hostelries in cities, towns, villages and suburbs. Now *Great Yorkshire Beer* is here to make that journey even more enjoyable and rewarding. So whether you undertake it on foot, by bus, car or on a bike or sometimes just from the comfort of your armchair, please enjoy it and all that Yorkshire's great craft brewers have to offer. Cheers!

Greg Mulholland MP
Chair, Parliamentary Save the Pub Group
One of CAMRA Top 40 Campaigners

Intro

In summer 2011, Tetley's – Leeds' most renowned brewer – closed its city-centre brewery, shifting production to the Midlands. Although owned by Carlsberg for some time, the loss of the brewery carried a real significance in Leeds. Despite the obvious loss to the cultural and economical landscape of the city, the closure gave the brewers left behind space to step out of the shadow of Tetley's, innovate and brew beer that the county can be proud of.

Although Yorkshire still has large breweries flying the flag for the county – most notably Keighley's Timothy Taylor and John Smith's of Tadcaster – the boom in independent brewing that is sweeping the sector as a whole has found Yorkshire to be a stronghold of brewing, in both sheer volume of breweries and creativity.

Just below the mid-size, established regional brewers such as Copper Dragon (Skipton), Black Sheep and Theakston's (Masham) sit a group of hard-working, passionate brewers, using regionality, originality and quality as a guide to brewing a uniquely Yorkshire pint. These brewers are using their smaller brewhouses to create supremely interesting and tasty beers.

Why are there so many breweries in Yorkshire? Some would say it's simply our heritage; we've always had beer. Not to have breweries dotted around our cities, towns and countryside would be anathema to a Yorkshireman. We are a proud lot, and want our own 'anything' – be it bakers, brewers or butchers – to be the best it can be.

Others would say that we've been lucky in many ways; that we have an inherent culture of beer and plenty of room for breweries and pubs to thrive. Our countryside is full of historic pubs waiting to be filled with beer. In bustling locations such as York, Leeds, Sheffield and Huddersfield our tradition of innovative brewing leads to established brewers supporting younger ones, cross-pollinating markets and leading to a truly vibrant beer culture that people travel to in order to experience.

One major influence – not only in the progression of independent brewing in Yorkshire but in the UK – was Dave Wickett. In 1981 he bought the Alma pub in Sheffield and decided, much against the norm, that he wanted as diverse a range of Real Ale that he could find for his customers. Renaming it the Fat Cat, Wickett made sure that – to the displeasure of some of his locals – one of his favourite beers, Timothy Taylor's iconic *Landlord Pale Ale*, was on the bar when he opened. This was a bold move at the time. The pub was a massive success, and went from strength to strength as a stronghold of Real Ale – not only in Sheffield, but in Yorkshire.

In 1990 he went one step further and set up Kelham Island, the first independent brewery in Sheffield for 100 years. A fruity, easy-drinking Pale Ale called *Pale Rider* became Kelham's most recognised beer, winning many, many awards. In the years since, independent brewing flourished in Sheffield and beyond. Dave swung the spotlight back onto what great beer is out there – once you hack your way through the jungle of major breweries – and he continued to work with microbrewers both in the UK and abroad.

Sadly, Dave passed away in early 2012 after a battle with bone cancer. His influence in brewing both in Sheffield, Yorkshire and the UK as a whole cannot be understated. Simply, he gave the industry a jolt and reminded people what they love about brewing – and drinking – Real Ale: independence, regionality, character and – most importantly – *flavour*.

The brewers featured in this book belong to a new generation, one that is as influenced by beer cultures overseas as much as in Yorkshire. Like the best artists, those influences are soaked up, mixed with personal history and taste, and emerge as something entirely new.

It's a handful of these brewers – working hard to make sure that Yorkshire beer is amongst the most innovative and unique beer in the UK – who are highlighted in this book.

Great Yorkshire Beer is not intended to be a definitive list. There are brewers everywhere in our fair county, and it would take a more sizeable book than this to list them all. Instead, I've profiled some of the younger breweries that I personally feel have really pushed the growth of Real Ale in the county in the last few years.

When I look at the breweries involved in this book, I see more than a group of people making a 'product' to sell. I see brewers who have changed their careers – at some risk – to do what they want to do. I see brewers embracing the next generation of drinkers, using food, social media and social events to connect with drinkers young and old, stepping out from behind the mash tun and connecting with their customers in a way that truly creates a bond between the customer and the artisan not seen in many other industries.

I see brewers forming partnerships and collaborating, brewing together and sharing knowledge. I see brewers with a thirst for innovation, forging ahead with one eye on the ever-changing landscape of beer. I see brewers looking to other nations – not to mention other counties – for inspiration. I see brewers whose simple wish is to own a clutch of pubs and ale-houses for you to enjoy their beer in the most perfect setting imaginable, cutting out the middle man. I see brewers who, quite simply, want to brew the best pint that they can for you to enjoy. All this, boiled down, into a pint of unique, supremely tasty Yorkshire beer.

We really do have a fantastic, eclectic mix of beers to choose from, and I hope this guide goes some way to inspiring a journey of your own – to discover a taste of Yorkshire.

Leigh Linley

Beer in the Dales

The Yorkshire Dales: ragged drystone walls, skipping springtime lambs and – of course – Yorkshire beer. There are countless pubs and inns dotted around our fair county, and there are plenty of smaller brewers in the region brewing tasty beers for you to quench your thirst after a long walk.

Here's a quick guide to a few that you'll want to keep an eye out for.

Dark Horse Brewery in Hetton (near Skipton) brew the famous *Hetton Pale Ale* – branded 'Yorkshire's Best Pint' in 2008 by a TV programme of the same name. Refreshingly fruity, with a creamy, malty body, it's the perfect restorative pint after a long walk. The Tempest Arms (Skipton) and The Bull (Broughton) are good places to catch it.

Cropton Brewery have been around since 1984, and has since grown a reputation for tasty, solid beers with a few seasonal surprises thrown in. *Monkman's Slaughter* – their scarily-named Strong Ale – is a winter favourite, and you can see where this and other beers such as *Yorkshire Moors* and *Two Pints* are brewed by visiting The New Inn. This picturesque pub/bed and breakfast near Pickering hosts a popular annual beer festival, and is the home of the brewery. Cropton is also the home of The Great Yorkshire Brewery, who produce an excellent Lager called (what else?) *Yorkshire Lager*.

Daleside are one of the region's bigger brewers, brewing their first beer in the mid 80s. Since then, Daleside's reputation for quality, unfussy beers has seen them become a massively popular choice for drinkers all over the region. *Blonde, Bitter* and *Special Bitter* have graced many a bar, and bottled favourites such as the powerful *Monkey Wrench*, *Ripon Jewel* and the lightly spiced *Morocco Ale* make Daleside a very, very popular choice.

The Yorkshire Dales Brewing Company brew a colourful, eclectic range of beers in styles from all over the world – Pilsners, Wheat Beers and Smoked Porters to name but three. Based in Askrigg, their beers have fans up and down the region, with the mysterious, devilishly oaky *Garsdale Smokebox* Porter being a personal favourite of mine. If it's something a little different you're after, the Yorkshire Dales Brewing Company is the one for you.

Nick Stafford's equine-themed **Hambleton Ales** have slowly grown into one of the region's most loved breweries since starting the brewery in 1991. Hambleton pioneered gluten-free brewing with both Ale and a Lager now available. Their Extra Stout Porter, *Nightmare*, is a multiple award-winner.

Since 2003, **Wensleydale Brewery** have produced tasty beers for the ramblers of the Dales to enjoy. Now popping up occasionally throughout Yorkshire, their popular range in both cask and bottle includes the excellent *Coverdale Poacher IPA* and *Black Dub Oat Stout*. Wensleydale have a firm and loyal following throughout the region. The light, crisp, *Semer Water Summer Ale* is perfect for those *very* occasional hot spells we get!

The Highest Pub in Yorkshire

Never mind Yorkshire, the Tan Hill Inn in the Dales is the highest in the UK! Sitting at 1732 feet above sea level, the Tan Hill will certainly reward those that scale the climb up to its door with home-cooked food and plenty of fortifying Real Ale.

CROPTON
Brewery
SINCE 1984
CORESB
STOUT
ALC 4.2% VOL
BOTTLE
CONDITIONED

The Brew Co
Sheffield

Pete Roberts began his career trading in a very different kind of vice. Working for Cadbury's for many years, it wasn't until he started managing networks for the chocolate behemoth that he realised he was in the wrong job.

'I ended up doing something that I never really set out to do,' he laments. As the company eventually jettisoned jobs to save money, Pete realised that, after 18 years, his job would eventually evaporate, too. He left the company with his master's degree, and did what any self-respecting Yorkshireman would do: went to the pub to consider his options over a comforting pint.

'I was having a beer and reading through the local CAMRA magazines,' he recalls, 'and at the bottom of one of the pages, I saw the Brewlab advert. *Why not run a brewery?* it said.' Inspired by his new-found freedom and with some financial means to launch a brewery – courtesy of a redundancy cheque – he got on the train to Sunderland and completed the Brewlab course.

Pete smiles as he recalls the few weeks. 'It was a short course, but I was hooked. I completed all the practical assignments, came home and put a business plan together – which I'd never done before.' Despite his inexperience, he must have done something right.

The Brew Co's site (where he's been since 2008) consists of three adjoining units, filled floor-to-ceiling with fermenting vessels, casks and his pine-clad kettle. Despite being one of the more modest of the group in this book, the brewery has a homely, cosy feel, and suits Pete down to the ground.

'It is compact, but when you brew on your own, you need everything at arm's-length!' he laughs, sighing the sigh of

Pete Roberts

many, many lone brewers out there, digging out malt, washing casks and keeping one eye on vigorously-boiling kettles, being the tough reality of brewing.

How did Pete formulate that initial roster of beers? I ask. 'In the beginning I wanted to have one of every style – simple as that. The first beer I brewed was a Best Bitter, which sold really well, as it happens. Pale followed, and I was supplying only to Sheffield initially. The first cask I sold was at The Riverside pub.'

Pete goes on to illustrate the typically straightforward way that he sold his first cask of Ale. 'I walked in, introduced myself as a new brewer, and asked if they'd take a cask of my new beer. They said "yes", to which I replied "Great. It's outside, in the back of the car!"' he laughs.

'I did the same at The Harlequin, and couldn't believe it. I came home and said to my partner, "I've done it! I've sold two casks!"' One suspects from the warmth of the story that Pete had not felt that kind of job satisfaction for some time.

'I had my business plan, of course, but at that point I just wanted to get my beer out there. I just wanted people to drink – and enjoy – what I'd brewed.'

Pete admits that since those days, the beer range has changed dramatically. Drinkers enjoying The Brew Co's beers enjoy a very different type of beer now to those first Pales and Bests, despite the two being popular choices in the alehouses of Sheffield.

'I was inexperienced in brewing, and I was more concerned about brewing what I thought people wanted to drink. You know, styles that you see a lot of. Since then, I've improved as a brewer, and I can brew what I want to brew – giving people choice.'

He also acknowledges that even since he's started brewing, the public taste has shifted. 'Even four years ago, you wouldn't really see some beers that are around now being drunk,' he says, referring to more esoteric styles that now litter the market such as Black IPAs and Saison. 'Brewers are more adventurous, the ingredients are better, and even new brewers are more focussed on flavour (rather than simply shifting volume) now.'

He points to one of his current beers as an example. 'I brewed an IPA called *Frontier* back then that people found too bitter, so I shelved it. A few weeks ago, I tried it again – purely on a whim – and after a little tweaking of the recipes, it's gone down a storm.' I can attest to the subtle, rolling bitterness of *Frontier*. It's a great IPA and perfectly illustrates the modern taste for Pale Ales to have a little more bite to them.

Pete is a well-travelled fellow, and his love of America is obvious. Spending time in places such as Portland (widely regarded as the home of independent brewing in the US), he really got his tastebuds wrapped around the 'American style'; their imaginative use of hops and focus on aroma rather than simple 'sessionability'.

The Brew Co's hop store illustrates that point; boxes of vacuum-packed hops are everywhere, mostly of US origin. They all combine with hops from the UK, New Zealand and Slovenia too, all ready to provide a refreshing, zippy lift to the malt profiles of Pete's beer.

However, make no mistake – The Brew Co's beers are not pastiches of American styles; they are true Yorkshire ales, always brewed with one eye on balance and drinkability.

Pete points to a recent addition to his range – the subtly-monikered *Hop Ripper* – as an example of what he likes to drink now. Beers with assertive, juicy hop character, but at a strength that allows the drinker to try more than one. Pete now considers his range a cornucopia of Pales alongside lush Porters and Stouts – even a popular Bock-style beer – as a more complete reflection of where he wants The Brew Co to be.

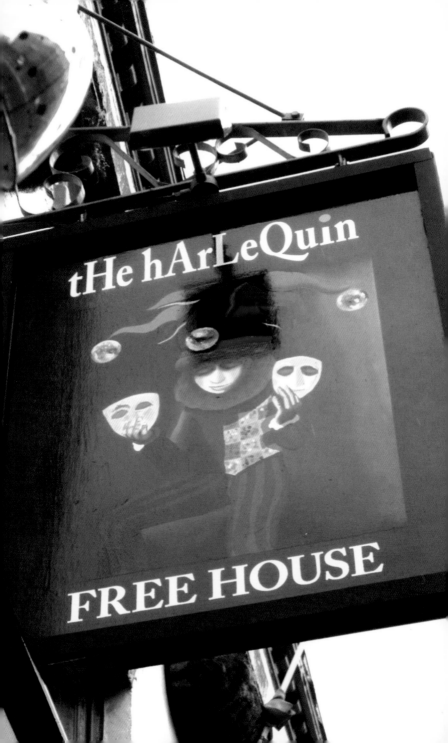

The Brew Co has also picked up a few awards along the way: 2010's *Hop Monster* won Gold at Sheffield's Steel City Beer Festival, an award that his *St Petrus Stout* did the year before. It would seem that despite the amount of established breweries in Sheffield, Pete is doing something right, holding his own in a city known for Real Ale and highly-regarded pubs.

In fact, it could be said that it is in pubs where The Brew Co's future lies: The Harlequin is run by Liz, Pete's fiancée, and the couple now live above it, keeping a keen eye on customers enjoying their beers.

'I started out supplying a monthly special to the pub, but they were so popular, they began buying everything we did.'

With The Harlequin garnering a reputation for quality Ales – and in particular The Brew Co's regular appearances – the subject of changing the ownership into something more formal eventually came up. Of course, this was helped with some gentle coaxing from Pete. 'We really liked the pub, and had done for a long time. I'd been badgering the landlady for a while to let me run the place, actually.'

The popularity of the new brewery's beers gave the then-owner enough confidence that Pete and Liz could do the job right. Pete saw the pub as the perfect platform for his beers, along with an always-rotating crop of locally-brewed Ales and bottled beers from around the world, as well as home-cooked, quality food and an excellent selection of Ciders and Rums (another passion of Pete's). The bar selection simply reflects Pete's taste as a lover of beer.

'Blonde and Best are the 'house beers' at The Harlequin,' he states. 'Both are incredibly popular.' I can see why. Both are excellent examples of the style – easy-going, smooth and delicately floral. I found that smooth, sweet body to be The Brew Co's defining characteristic – no matter how assertive the finish, they are incredibly easy-going beers.

As we sit in The Harlequin, blues music gently lilting in the background, I'd say that Pete and Liz have certainly achieved their original plan for the place. It's a pub for everyone. As we walk in, Pete greets and chats amiably to a regular, and makes a point of thanking everyone who leaves during our stop for dropping by.

'The food's got to be important. Simple things like house-cooked chips, quality, hand-made burgers, beer-battered onion rings. And a good pint,' he laughs, not forgetting the bigger picture. Pete's point is a simple one, but one that seems lost on many pub-owners looking to provide an experience: the food doesn't have to be complicated – just honest, and home-made.

Perhaps The Harlequin's double-sided 'Happy and Sad' sign, swinging against a typically gun-metal Sheffield sky, illustrates the two sides to both the pub and The Brew Co as an entity: a brewery and pub for all; and inclusive yet entirely individual to those who drink in her.

The **Brew** Company

BLONDE
PALE, HOPPY, FRUITY

4% ABV

The **Brew** Company

Frontier

IPA
Pale • Bitter • Hoppy

4.7% ABV

Blonde Abv: 4.2%

Shimmering gold in colour, with a tight, cloud-white head, *Blonde* is a perfect restorative pint. Sweet and smooth in the body with a floral aroma full of elderflower and just a hint of honey. *Blonde* finishes green, grassy and only subtly bitter.

Try it with: pan-fried fish, spiced chicken, turkey stir-fry

Frontier Abv: 4.7%

A true session IPA, with a nose full of tropical fruit and straw-like notes. Pale amber in colour, with an almost vanilla-sponge note in the body – which is full and robust. The finish is long, with pine-needle and citrus pithiness combining to provide a rolling, fresh finish.

Try it with: roast belly pork, BBQ ribs, smoked meat pizza

St Petrus Abv: 5%

Straight-up, no-nonsense Stout from Sheffield. The aromatic nose is heavy with bitter chocolate and roasted coffee notes. Those notes carry through to sweet, thick body, where they mingle with dark cherry and hints of raisin. *St Petrus* finishes dry with that espresso note coming to the fore.

Try it with: burger with blue cheese and smoked bacon, chocolate cheesecake, steak and kidney pudding

Tasty Taster

Fried Mozzarella

Here's a tasty, Italian-inspired lunch that is wonderful with a glass of cool, bitter Pale Ale or a soft, fruity Blonde. Under a pre-heated grill, melt a large knob of butter with a slug of olive oil in a griddle pan. Cut slices of bloomer loaf and lightly toast both sides in the butter under the grill, and remove.

Lay slices of mozzarella cheese, Yorkshire ham, tomato and a few leaves of fresh basil on top, and then place under the grill for five minutes or so to melt. When melted, put your top slice of bread on, flip the sandwich back into the pan, and toast the other side. Sprinkle salt and black pepper on top, and enjoy warm with a salad.

CAMRA

Formed in 1971, CAMRA are an independent consumer organisation devoted to the promotion and preservation of Real Ale in the UK. Yorkshire has many branches, and if you really want to support Cask Ale, then join up. CAMRA often organise trips to breweries and social events – which are great ways to get 'behind the scenes' at your local breweries.

Sheffield: Valley of Beer

Sheffield is one of Yorkshire's hotspots for beer. It has the famous 'Valley of Beer' crawl lying at the heart of it. Sheffield has the right mix of traditional, long-standing pubs – who remain fiercely independent – and buzzy, modern bars and gastropubs that are attracting new audiences to beer.

There are far too many pubs for me to list here – but here are a few pubs close to the city centre that you definitely don't want to miss. If you love Real Ale and Craft Beer, then Sheffield is one place you *have* to visit.

The Sheffield Tap

Standing proudly on platform one at Sheffield Train Station, you can't miss The Sheffield Tap. As with the 'Tap' at York, you can expect a vast array of beers from Yorkshire and further afield adorning the elegant, mahogany bar. Prepare to miss your train. This is one stop you won't want to get off at.

The Harlequin

The Brew Co's unofficial tap, The Harlequin, serves more than just regular Ales from nearby breweries. There's plenty of Cider and American bottled beers to choose from, as well as a hearty range of home-cooked food to soak it all up.

The Fat Cat

Since opening in 1981, The Fat Cat has carved out a legendary status for itself amongst Yorkshire's drinkers. The spiritual home of Kelham Island Brewery, expect up to 11 Real Ales to choose from – 4 of which will be from Kelham Island itself.

The Kelham Island Tavern

A multiple CAMRA award-winner and perennial favourite of Sheffield's hordes of beer fans. Close to The Fat Cat, it's another pub where the emphasis is on the region's excellent Cask Ales, with a dash of folk music thrown in.

The Gardeners Rest

After bouncing back from the floods of 2007, The Rest has become the best place to try out beers from The Sheffield Brewery Company. Expect to find the likes of the refreshing *Blanco Blonde* and the satisfying *Sheffield Porter* on the bar.

The Wellington

The little pub with a big heart. Home of Little Ale Cart Brewing, The Wellington has a reputation for serving local Ales in excellent condition, with friendly, enthusiastic staff. Amongst others, expect to find offerings from Little Ale Cart, Millstone and Bradford's Salamander on the bar.

The Devonshire Cat

Popular with students, the Devonshire is a large, open-plan pub with an excellent array of beers from established Yorkshire brewers such as Abbeydale, Bradfield and Acorn as well as a wide range of bottled beers from around the world. A city centre favourite with plenty of atmosphere.

THE

Ilkley

BREWERY Co.

Ilkley Brewery
Ilkley

Ilkley: one of Yorkshire's most loved spa towns. Nestling under the iconic shadow of the Cow and Calf Rocks, it seems like the perfect setting for a brewery – one who brews robust, hearty Ales to slake the thirst of the thousands of walkers who traverse the celebrated moors and drink in its taverns on a daily basis.

Indeed, historically it did have: The Ilkley Brewery and Aerated Water Company, which was founded in 1873. Supplying its trademark 'Olicana' (which was the Roman name for Ilkley) branded beers and waters, it grew into one of the largest breweries in Yorkshire before being taken over by Hammond's Bradford Brewery Co in 1923. Parts of the old brewery building still stood until only recently. Breweriana bearing the Olicana trademark can still be seen in some of the town's pubs.

The closure of the brewery left a hole in Ilkley's heritage – until recently. Although Chris Ives and Stewart Ross had initially met through working in commercial property, the pair got to know one another better when, in 1999, Stewart joined the Ilkley & District Round Table. A shared passion for Real Ale gave birth to the incredibly popular Ilkley Beer Festival in 2008, serving not only as an excellent showcase for local beers but raising thousands of pounds for charity.

'The idea (for the brewery) really came to life whilst working with brewers from the festival,' smiles Stewart. 'I realised this was such a rewarding, friendly industry to get involved in. I wanted that; to work at something that I could enjoy.'

Chris felt much the same way and the pair started work on breathing life into the concept of a new Ilkley Brewery. After securing financial support, Chris and Stewart took the plunge. Leaving their roles in property, The Ilkley Brewery was born in January 2009. At this point, they couldn't have imagined how successful their venture would be.

As spring sprung across the moor, Chris and Stewart took a couple of crash courses in brewing. Their first brewery – an eight-barrel brew plant – was situated in the Lencia Trading Estate. Shortly thereafter, their maiden beer was brewed: the light, summery *Olicana Gold*, with the first pint being sold at The Junction pub in nearby Baildon. *Olicana Gold* was a success, and Ilkley Brewery's first permanent pumps soon popped up at The Wheatley Arms in Ben Rhydding and at Market Town Tavern's *Bar T'at* in Ilkley.

The sprightly *Olicana Gold* was soon joined by *Ilkley Original*: a darker, richly full-bodied beer, but one which retained a fresh, fruity aroma. 'We put a lot of hops in there, despite it being a little maltier,' explains Stewart. 'From the outset, we wanted flavour in our beers. We got sick of going to beer festivals and seeing gallons of "light, hoppy session beer" with nothing behind them.' This overriding ethos of full-bodied malt, topped with plenty of hops to provide wonderful aroma, soon became Ilkley's signature style.

Richard Shelton joined Stewart and Chris as a drayman, but they soon realised that his skills were more than that of a driver. 'Every time he delivered beer, he came back with an order!' Stewart laughs. 'He became our sales director not long after that, and he now has an equal stake in the brewery.'

Ilkley's wholesome beers were slowly gaining fans through Yorkshire, but it was a beer named after a famous Yorkshire lass that really powered Ilkley to the top of the local brewing tree. Widely regarded as their flagship beer, *Mary Jane* has rapidly become one of the most highly-regarded Pale Ales that the region produces. It's no surprise. *Mary Jane* remains one of Yorkshire brewing's true modern classics. Juicy, thirst-quenching and packed with fruit-bowl aroma. '*Mary Jane*'s success enabled us to shoehorn more money into the business because it had such momentum behind it,' explains Stewart. Hitting upon the recipe for *Mary Jane*, it seems, was

From left: Chris Ives,
Richard Shelton,
Stewart Ross

a real lightning-in-a-bottle moment for the brewery.

From that point onwards, it seemed Ilkley went from strength to strength, picking up award after award from beer festivals and an excellent double SIBA (Society of Independent Brewers) win for *Mary Jane*. The citrusy, sunny beer even appeared on the bar at the House of Commons.

In early 2011, the brewery moved to a new 2,600 sq ft brewery on Ashlands Road. The modern, 20 barrel plant enables the brewery to produce over 20,000 pints a week and goes some way to ensuring that the loyal following both locally and nationally that Chris and Stewart have built up get their fix of Ilkley's beers. In summer 2011, the brewery took the interesting step of opening its doors every month to the public with a night of food (from local food hero Lishman's Butchers) super-fresh beer and local entertainment. The Beer Society is already becoming a firm favourite, and busier with every passing month.

So, have Chris and Stewart achieved what they set out to do? Are they brewing the beers they wanted to when they stood behind the bar at the Ilkley Beer Festival?

'The feedback we get is that people look for our beers because they trust the name; but they aren't traditional beers. We wanted to reflect the heritage of the town, certainly, but brew interesting beers,' says Chris. The formula works; there's no doubt about that. Ilkley Brewery have become one of Yorkshire's most decorated – and popular – brewers in an incredibly short space of time.

That questing nature – Ilkley's ability to remain relevant and not fall into the trap of simply being labelled a 'Traditional Brewer' – led to two recent additions to their roster. Wanting to see how their beers tasted dispensed by keg – and therefore reaching another audience – the 'Artisan' range was launched. Rather than try and fit their existing cask range into the new system, they brewed specifically for it: a version of *Mary Jane* (renamed *MJ*) joining *Fortis Stout* and *MJ*

Summit (a rich, sweet, American-style Pale Ale with a citrus finish). The range has started promisingly, and *Fortis Stout* in particular is proving incredibly popular across the country. '*Fortis* has replaced *Guinness* in eight London bars,' smiles Chris, clearly proud of usurping the ubiquitous Stout.

Perhaps more significantly, Ilkley launched the 'Origins' range in early 2012: a platform for limited-edition collaboration brewing and experimental batches. 'Eventually we may even have two distinct breweries under one banner. With Origins we will brew our interpretations of classic styles from around the world: Pilsner, Wheat Beer, Light Ale,' Chris confirms. So far, Origins has given birth to collaborations with beer writers Pete Brown (*Medina*; a Saison with a twist of Moroccan spice) and Melissa Cole (*Siberia*; another Saison – spiked with Yorkshire forced rhubarb, vanilla and grains of paradise), and a new IPA named *The Chief*. These beers have been received with incredible positivity both in Yorkshire and further afield.

Despite their local popularity, new markets are opening up for Ilkley all the time – and business is good. 'People still want to discover us. What's great for us is that when they do, they tend to want more. That's because of the quality of our range,' says Chris.

Ilkley Brewery are a brewery that keep one eye on tradition – the sole brewer in Ilkley would be stupid not to – and one eye on the future, innovating their beer upwards and onwards with new styles and looking at different ways of reaching their audience. More food nights – and maybe even a pub or two – are on their radar, and I'm sure that they will appear in the not-too-distant future.

Stewart Ross left the brewery in early 2013 to pursue other brewing interests. Chris and Richard, alongside their brewing team, are forging ahead with increasing Ilkley's reach both in the UK and abroad, with export to the US firmly in their sights. Given their love for brewing and local pride, you get the impression that there's nothing that the Ilkley Brewery can't achieve.

Ilkley Brewery Co Ltd

Ashlands Rd, Ilkley LS29 8JT

www.ilkleybrewery.co.uk

Mary Jane

Straw-hued Pale Ale, with an aroma of lemon and lime and with a zesty finish that echoes lemon sherbets. Supremely thirst-quenching, *Mary Jane* is Ilkley's flagship beer – and rightly so.

Abv: 3.9%

Try it with: Thai curries, coconut-battered prawns, shellfish

Stout Mary

Smooth Oat Stout: brown-black in colour, with a sweet, chocolate-led heart at the middle, finishing slightly sweet. Surprisingly light and well-balanced for the abv, *Stout Mary* is a lighter interpretation of the style.

Abv: 4.5%

Try it with: hazelnut cake, beef stew, smoked bacon and black pudding

Ilkley Pale (4.2%abv)

The use of Nelson Sauvin hops in this bright, lively beer make *Ilkley Pale* a real thirst-quencher. *Pale* has masses of grapefruit and lime notes on the nose, and a long, drying finish with more pink grapefruit.

Abv: 4.2%

Try it with: Key lime pie, chicken korma, barbecued pineapple

Tasty Taster

Soy and Honey Chicken Goujons

For a sweet/salty snack with an oriental feel, these soy and honey chicken goujons are a winner. Simply slice some chicken breast fillets into strips, and marinate overnight in dark soy sauce, a chopped clove of garlic, a twist of black pepper, a little chopped ginger and one small chopped chilli. If you have any five-spice seasoning, you could use that, too.

When you are ready to eat, heat your grill to high and arrange them on a baking sheet. Make a glaze with runny honey, more dark soy sauce (about half as much as the honey) and a tiny splash of sesame oil. Grill the chicken, basting every five minutes, slowly building up that glaze. They'll take about 15 minutes, and taste surprisingly good with Stout or Dark Milds such as Ilkley's *Black*.

Kirkstall Brewery
Leeds

KIRKSTALL
BREWERY

'I was fascinated by the history of Kirkstall; there's such a long brewing tradition in the area and I felt that it ought to be revived,' says Steve Holt. 'When I decided to set up a brewery, I tried really hard to find a location in Kirkstall. We couldn't set up anywhere else and call ourselves Kirkstall Brewery.'

Steve is clearly a man who, when he sets his mind to something, gets it done. As a long-time enthusiast of all things beer, he has amassed a vast amount of knowledge about breweries long consigned to the history books – particularly in Leeds. The oft-neglected history of the original Kirkstall Brewery – first set up in the mid-1800s and owned by Dutton's of Blackburn and Whitbread amongst others through the years – loomed large in his mind when he decided to join the fraternity of brewing.

'Of all the Leeds breweries, I was most fascinated by the story of Kirkstall Brewery. The whole area is fascinating; there's even a tenuous brewing link to the Abbey – although there's no solid proof that the monks there brewed!' No proof, but given that it housed Cistercian monks – an order being known for brewing in other regions – it's a fair assumption that the once-glorious Abbey could well have been filled with the comforting scent of steeping barley.

Steve is not a brewer by trade. At the end of an expansive career in brewery marketing and distribution he set up Vertical Drinks, the drinks importer which is credited with being at the vanguard of bringing Craft beers from America to the bars and pubs of the UK. Initially working with Safeway, he brought the superlative Sierra Nevada *Pale Ale* into the UK in 2003 – and the rest is history. North Leeds' famous Beer Bar, largely credit their relationship with Steve and

Vertical in helping them establish their nation-wide reputation as an altar of beer worship.

This wasn't enough, however. Steve wanted to be involved at the start of the supply chain, rather than the end. He wanted his own brewery, and to become part of the history of brewing in the region that he'd spent so much time reading about.

Given the geographical constraints he had set out, it took a while to find a site, but once one was secured, Steve enlisted the help of Dave Sanders to be his brewmaster. Although he keeps a low profile, Dave is undoubtedly one of the region's brewing heroes. He cut his teeth at the infamous Feast & Firkin brewpub in Leeds, and recalls fondly visiting Tetley's Brewery for the odd technical brewing lesson – the only formal training he ever took.

The spell ended, however, when Punch Taverns took over the chain and Dave was promptly made redundant. After a spell heading up West Yorkshire Brewery at Luddenden Foot, the brewery joined forces with nearby Elland Brewery. It was at Elland that Dave really came into his own as a brewer, refining his recipe for the multiple award-winning *1873 Porter*, amongst others. The ruby-hued, Victorian-style Porter is widely regarded as one of the country's best examples of the style, and is still referred to in hushed tones even after Dave's departure.

Steve got to know Dave over the years through the Great British Beer Festival. Such is Dave's standing in the beer community that he has supervised the American Beer stand of the festival since 2001 – and this meant sourcing some of the beer through Vertical Drinks.

When the call came, Dave was more than happy to join Steve in his mission to resurrect brewing in Kirkstall. 'We sat down and I realised, "Yeah, I can do this." It seemed like an exciting opportunity,' smiles Dave.

Opportunity it was. The duo set about formulating the beers;

the names had already been dreamt up by Steve, and Dave was tasked with bringing them to life. Dave oversees all aspects of brewing, keeping long hours in order to make sure every batch he brews is to his liking. He's meticulous and constantly trying to brew the absolute best beer that he can.

'As a brewer, I'm looking for goosebumps when I taste one of my beers,' asserts Dave, admitting that it's the pursuit of that *magic moment* that keeps him going. That's the benchmark that Dave sets for himself – and therefore Kirkstall.

Sanders' craftsmanship is evident in all of Kirkstall's relatively small regular range of beer: from the luscious *Black Band Porter*, awash with subtle liquorice and smoke, to *Kirkstall Pale Ale*, *Three Swords* (each sword represents a hop) and the heady *Dissolution IPA* (with a nod in the name to Kirkstall's monastical link). Another beer, *BYB*, has recently been added to the line-up – another link from Steve to a cult Leeds brewer of bygone times.

'*BYB* is actually named after Bentley's Yorkshire Breweries (who were based in Woodlesford from 1893 onwards), although we call it Best Yorkshire Bitter. Their livery is actually on our pump clip,' Steve laughs. 'Quite a few of our customers really wanted a beer that was a little lower in alcohol, so they could enjoy a few more.'

Kirkstall's range is deliberately small so that they can concentrate on quality – but that's not to say that Kirkstall don't brew the odd one-off. In the past year or so, they've collaborated with Odell Brewing of Colorado, resulting in *Aquitaine*, a rich Old Ale matured in Bordeaux casks. Recently they brewed a special edition of their IPA – adding rye to the recipe to create a spicier, nuttier malt backbone to the beer.

When I ask Dave what beer he's most proud of creating, he gives a typically democratic answer. 'It depends what mood I'm in!' he laughs. We chat about Kirkstall's style, and Dave

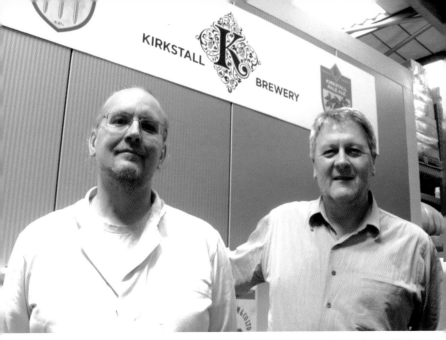

From left: Dave Sanders, Steve Holt

is keen to point out the importance of malt in his creations. 'Texture-wise, there's a lot going on. Malt is part of your artist's palette, and I like to create multi-faceted beers with a lot of body, a lot of character.'

In terms of Kirkstall's reach, don't expect to see them spread too far and wide. At the moment, Steve simply isn't that interested in sending casks all over the country, as he believes his beer is inextricably tied to his industrious suburb of Leeds.

This strategy might not seem like good business, but it works. People simply have to travel to Leeds to try Kirkstall's beer – and this creates a sense of provenance and locality. Kirkstall's fans have a keen sense of loyalty, and a sense of comfort comes from knowing that when you get that urge for a *Kirkstall Pale Ale*, you know where to find it – and that a 'bad' pint of it is rarely served.

'I'd rather have fewer outlets that can always get our beer, rather than spreading out all over the place. If we can get local people supporting us and enjoying our beer, then that gives us a really solid base to build upon,' Steve continues. 'The majority of our beer stays in Yorkshire, and that's the best way to supply good, fresh beer to people.' Kirkstall Brewery support local causes and maintain a high profile socially, sponsoring beer festivals and popping up at food events and charity days.

So what sets Kirkstall apart from the myriad other breweries in West Yorkshire? Steve does acknowledge that there is competition for space in Leeds in terms of brewing, but feels that Kirkstall has a slight edge in terms of the name alone. 'There are a lot of brewers in the region, yes. But what we've focussed on is our area. The old Kirkstall Brewery still stands – although as a halls of residence – and the name is well-known to the older generation as well as the young.'

So, whether you're born and bred in Leeds, or simply passing through, Kirkstall Brewery is there to give you a glimpse of the past – and a taste of the future – of brewing in Kirkstall.

Kirkstall Brewery

Wyther Lane, Kirkstall, LS5 3BT

www.kirkstallbrewerycompany.com

Black Band Porter Abv: 5.5%

Near-black in colour, *Black Band Porter* is one to savour. Beneath the creamy, tan head sits a rich Porter with bitter chocolate and roasted coffee notes up front that mingle with soft touches of oak, toasted brown bread, plummy fruit and vanilla as the sip goes on. The finish is crisper than you'd expect, but the overall feel is that of an incredibly satisfying Porter.

Try it with: blue cheese and leek quiche, cherry chocolate brownie, BBQ spare ribs

Dissolution IPA Abv: 5%

A classically-minded English IPA; amber in colour and a rounded, full body loaded with sweet malts and honey. There's pine-needle on the nose, and the finish is fruity with a rising, lasting bitterness rather than an all-out hop attack. Warming alcohol makes a fleeting appearance after the sip.

Try it with: beef satay, fried whitebait with lemon aioli, duck-liver pâté

Three Swords Abv: 4.5%

That classic Kirkstall malt profile is there in the body: sweet, golden malts – like digestive biscuits topped with honey – but the nose and finish is all tropical fruit. Pineapple and peach abound on the nose, and the finish is long, light and dry with lemon pith and apricot. Incredibly easy drinking.

Try it with: chicken Caesar salad, spiced bean fajitas, mild/soft cheeses

Spanish Tortilla

For an easy tapas-style starter or snack, Spanish tortilla is hard to beat. Chop an onion and a red pepper, then gently sauté in olive oil. Whilst this is cooking, slice a few small potatoes and parboil them. When firm but cooked, drain and set to one side to cool. Do the same with the onion and red pepper.

When cool, mix your veggies with four beaten eggs, and a big handful of chopped, fresh coriander. Heat a large glug of olive oil in a heavy pan, and slide the mixture into the hot oil. When the bottom of the tortilla is cooked, place the pan under a hot grill for 7-10 minutes to cook the top. Slide out onto a plate to cool, and then refrigerate – I think this dish tastes much better cold. Crack open a chilled Pale Ale and enjoy.

The Oldest Pub in Yorkshire

The Bingley Arms is, in fact, one of the oldest pubs in Britain, with a known history of having brewing premises since at least 953 AD. Located in Bardsey (near Leeds), the pub was a popular stop for travelling monks on their way to Kirkstall Abbey, and acquired its current name after being bought by Lord Bingley in 1780. It still stands today, serving fine food and – of course – ales, to modern-day thirsty travellers.

LEEDS BREWERY'S

LEODIS

·PREMIUM·LEEDS·LAGER·

Leeds Brewery
Leeds

Sam Moss and Michael Brothwell may have been born and raised in the south of England, but it was through drinking in the bustling pubs of York that they became enchanted with Ale. 'Pubs are such amazing places,' beams Sam as we chat in the bar of his own – The Midnight Bell, in Leeds.

The pair met whilst studying at York University. Seeking work, both ended up at York Brewery, where they tried their hand at pretty much every task a busy, productive brewery has to offer – sales, bar work, rudimentary brewing and – of course – cleaning.

The friends noticed that the beers on offer in York were becoming increasingly varied. All of a sudden, the ubiquitous pumpclips of Black Sheep and Tetley's were being joined by interesting, new breweries vying for a place in the drinkers' hearts. Inspired, they felt that they could – and *should* – try their hand at joining this group of newcomers.

Of course, money to do this was an issue – until a regular at one of the pubs that Sam worked in announced that he was selling his house. Sam and Michael bought it, renovated it, and sold it on, using the profit as the basis of their fighting fund. However, this meant that York would have to remain where they lived for the time being – and there were no real possibilities for a brewery site in the area. They would have to look further afield.

Despite being an obvious choice, Leeds was initially dismissed as Sam and Michael both assumed that it must have had an independent brewery of its own with the Leeds moniker. 'We couldn't believe it when we realised it didn't,' Sam laughs. 'Then again, historically, what would have been the point? Tetley's owned everything.'

Sam and Michael's early business plan was simple, yet amazingly ambitious for such a young brewery. 'We wanted to get every pub with a Leeds postcode to stock our beer. Not only that, but we wanted to open our own pubs – one a year, actually.'

After a year or so of planning and securing further funding, Leeds Brewery officially opened in summer 2007 in Holbeck, near the city centre. One thing was clear in Sam's mind from the start: the two of them could not bring their blueprint to life alone. 'Michael and I could brew. We could run pubs. We could sell beer. But we can't do it all, and do it well. We'd rather work with someone really, really good at those things for the good of the Brewery.'

Appointing a brewer, in that case, was a crucial step for the friends. They contacted Edinburgh's Heriot-Watt University – a hub for brewing students and mine of as-yet-untapped talent – asking if they knew of any graduates who would be open to heading up brewing operations.

Venkatesh Iyer's name cropped up; a friendly, vivacious young man who had relocated from Mumbai to study at Herriot-Watt. He was interviewed and summarily appointed. 'Venkatesh is someone who shared our vision straight away. He was the same age as us, and we wanted to be a young, vibrant brewery. He understood what we were trying to achieve. He ticked all the boxes, and became very important to us as a brewery.'

Venkatesh, Sam and Michael created the core range of *Leeds Pale*, *Best* and *Midnight Bell* (a strong Dark Mild Ale) simply out of the desire to have an unfussy, tasty beer in the light, mid-strength and dark categories. Despite *Pale*'s popularity, *Leeds Best* was the first success, with *Pale* suffering many teething problems, both in terms of taste, colour and condition. 'We had to get rid of four brews' worth of *Pale* before we were happy. It's such a vital beer to us. We really had to get it right – no matter how problematic it was to brew.'

Sam Moss

Those three beers (*Leeds Pale* in particular) were brewed not only to satisfy the ideals of the young brewers, but to attain popular status. These were beers for everyone in Leeds; beers for everyone in Yorkshire. 'Our beers are commercial, mainstream beers,' Sam admits, with no hesitation. 'We don't really do left-field. We simply want to brew beers that people want to drink more than one of.'

That unfussy, back-to-basics approach ran to the design of the brewery's logo, too. Years on, the pumpclips remain instantly recognisable on the bar. 'We didn't spend a great deal of money on that, but at the same time we wanted to do a good job and perhaps look bigger than we actually were.'

The boys worked with a local designer, who struck upon the distinctive 'Oval' logo for the brewery. Sam reveals that it's actually an abstract ear of barley, turned upwards. 'People see it and immediately know it's us.'

The Midnight Bell Team with Jamie Oliver (Leeds Brewery)

Despite Sam's assertion, as brewers (being creative people) generally will, Leeds do experiment from time to time. They installed a trial brewery upstairs at The Brewery Tap and from that produced *Leodis* – a crisp, thirst-quenching lager – as well as dabbling in other European beer styles such as Saison, Wheat and Dunkel beers. In late 2010 they produced *Gyle 479*, a sumptuous Stout aged in whisky barrels. Leeds do brew seasonal beers, but only as a quarterly indulgence, such is the focus on the core range.

With the beers flowing, the hard graft came: cold-calling, offering samples, engaging landlords and getting Leeds' beer into people's hands. They found pubs to be generally open to supporting the fledgling brewers. 'I think the brewery's name had a lot to do with the success!' Sam chuckles. 'People from Leeds are proud of where they are from and although they may not shout about it, they enjoy seeing *Leeds Pale* on the bar.'

Sam's point certainly resonates with me personally, being a Leodensian. Leeds is a proud, industrious city with rich sporting links (only one football club, rugby league and county cricket), and wondrous civic buildings. It feels like a city that punches above its weight, and that attitude is certainly reflected in Leeds Brewery.

When talk turns to Leeds' pub estate, Sam is clearly proud of the efforts of the team.

'Our pubs are what genuinely set us apart from our colleagues in brewing,' he beams. 'From the very beginning, we didn't want to be just a brewer. In fact, we found the site for The Midnight Bell (Holbeck, Leeds) before the brewery.'

Only planning and building delays meant the brewery and the flagship pub didn't open at the same time; which was – with typical ambition – the original intention.

'Our brewery isn't set up for tours, or even entertaining, really. Instead, we can take customers or interested parties to the pub, where we can better encapsulate what we are about: the beer, the cellar, the food, the staff, the setting. The Midnight Bell is a beautiful pub. We want our customers to want to come back. And our customers are everyone.'

It certainly works. I quickly glance across the bar. It's Saturday lunchtime, and it's nicely filling up with pre-match drinkers, bringing the volume level up a notch. There are diners in the snugs and at the tables unwrapping scarves and coats, clutching golden pints and perusing menus, settling in for a fortifying weekend brunch. 'We'll have the post-work crowd in, the football, rugby and cricket fans, and then we'll have the families and diners in,' says Sam, clearly pleased with the mix of people choosing to drink and eat with Leeds Brewery.

Talk turns to food, and the pub's recent visit by Jamie Oliver

(as part of his *Jamie's Great Britain* series), who left impressed with both the quality and locality of what was on offer – both on the bar and the plate. 'We brew beer with care, passion and exacting standards. Our chefs and staff work incredibly hard to serve the best food we can. Why should you pay attention to our beer if we send you out a microwaved lasagne to enjoy it with – and vice versa?'

Leeds Brewery's pubs have another common link: from the White Swan (sitting underneath the City Varieties), to the Garden Gate and the Midnight Bell, all are buildings which have strong emotional connections to Leeds' past. For Leeds Brewery to breathe new life into them seems too picture-perfect to be true.

'We've been lucky with the pubs that we have. The Garden Gate was such a find, we couldn't let it disappear. The White Swan was going downhill, and we managed to get that, too. We take pride in working with these buildings. The Garden Gate is one of the most important pubs, architecturally and emotionally, in the north of England.'

There's a care taken with the Garden Gate, in particular. The building is listed, and the only one not in the centre of Leeds. 'We were blown away when we visited it,' Sam laughs, echoing the sentiment that many who visit it for the first time say. 'It's a beautiful, beautiful pub, that's been enjoyed for years. We can't be 'the Brewery for Leeds' without being involved in pubs like the Garden Gate.'

It's not lost on Sam that these aspects of contributing to life in Leeds in a bigger way than just beer is something that, in its heyday, Tetley's would have done. Sam smiles broadly as he sums it up in one statement:

'It's about being part of the city. We are doing our job if people consider our beer to be their beer. That's what people in Leeds used to do with Tetley's. If you visited the city, you drank Tetley's. That's where we want to be – and maybe in 200 years' time, we might be!'

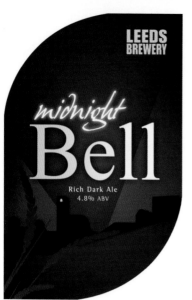

LEEDS
BREWERY

midnight
Bell

Rich Dark Ale
4.8% ABV

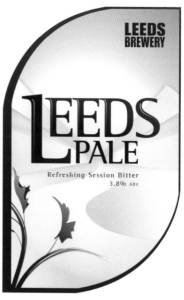

LEEDS
BREWERY

LEEDS
PALE

Refreshing Session Bitter
3.8% ABV

Leeds Brewery

3 Sydenham Road, Leeds, LS11 9RU

www.leedsbrewery.co.uk

Leeds Best Abv: 4.3%

A tawny Best Bitter, *Leeds Best* has a firm, creamy body and a dry, floral finish. Simple, moreish, refreshing and satisfying; a no-nonsense beer from a no-nonsense brewer.

Try it with: fish and chips, roasted pork, honey-roasted root vegetables

Midnight Bell Abv: 4.8%

As dark as midnight in winter, the brewery describes *Midnight Bell* as a Dark Mild, but there's a lot of body and strength here. Smooth, fruity notes of bitter chocolate and wheaten biscuit abound in the body, topped off with a sharp coffee note and just a hint of woodsmoke in the finish. A supremely easy-drinking beer despite its relative strength.

Try it with: steamed fruit puddings, tomato-based curries, oysters, grilled prawns

Leeds Pale Abv: 3.8%

Leeds' flagship Pale Ale is widely loved and consumed by the gallon in Leeds. With such an easy-going personality, it's no surprise. The palest of gold, sweet at first then drying to a finish laced with lemon and grapefruit, it's a beer that disappears all too quickly – especially when drunk in the summer sun.

Try it with: scampi and calamari, roast chicken, lemon cheesecake

Prawn Chorizo

Leeds Brewery also brew a refreshing, summery Pale Ale called *Hellfire* (4.8% abv). It's crisp and floral, and has more of a lager-esque profile than *Leeds Pale*. Don't miss out if you see it – especially during the summer months. If you're after a gloriously sunny meal, get your hands on the largest prawns you can find – with their shells on if possible.

Slice the prawns down the middle with a sharp knife, clean them up a little, and place under a red-hot grill for five minutes. When that sweet flesh is white, you're ready.

While this is grilling, throw some chopped Yorkshire Chorizo into a dry pan. Gently fry the chunks off – *but don't burn them* – and then pour the whole lot over the prawns. The flavour is in that orange oil; that's what chorizo is all about. Crack open a chilled *Hellfire* and relax. Wonderful.

Brewpubs

Brewpubs are not as popular as they used to be, but there remain a few in Yorkshire that do brew their own beer. The Fox and Newt, in Leeds, has a long history of brewing, and is currently home to Burley Street Brewhouse. The Brewery Tap, owned by Leeds Brewery, has a small brewery upstairs where various 'specials' are brewed. In Huddersfield, The Sportsman and The Rat and Ratchet have both recently begun brewing on premises.

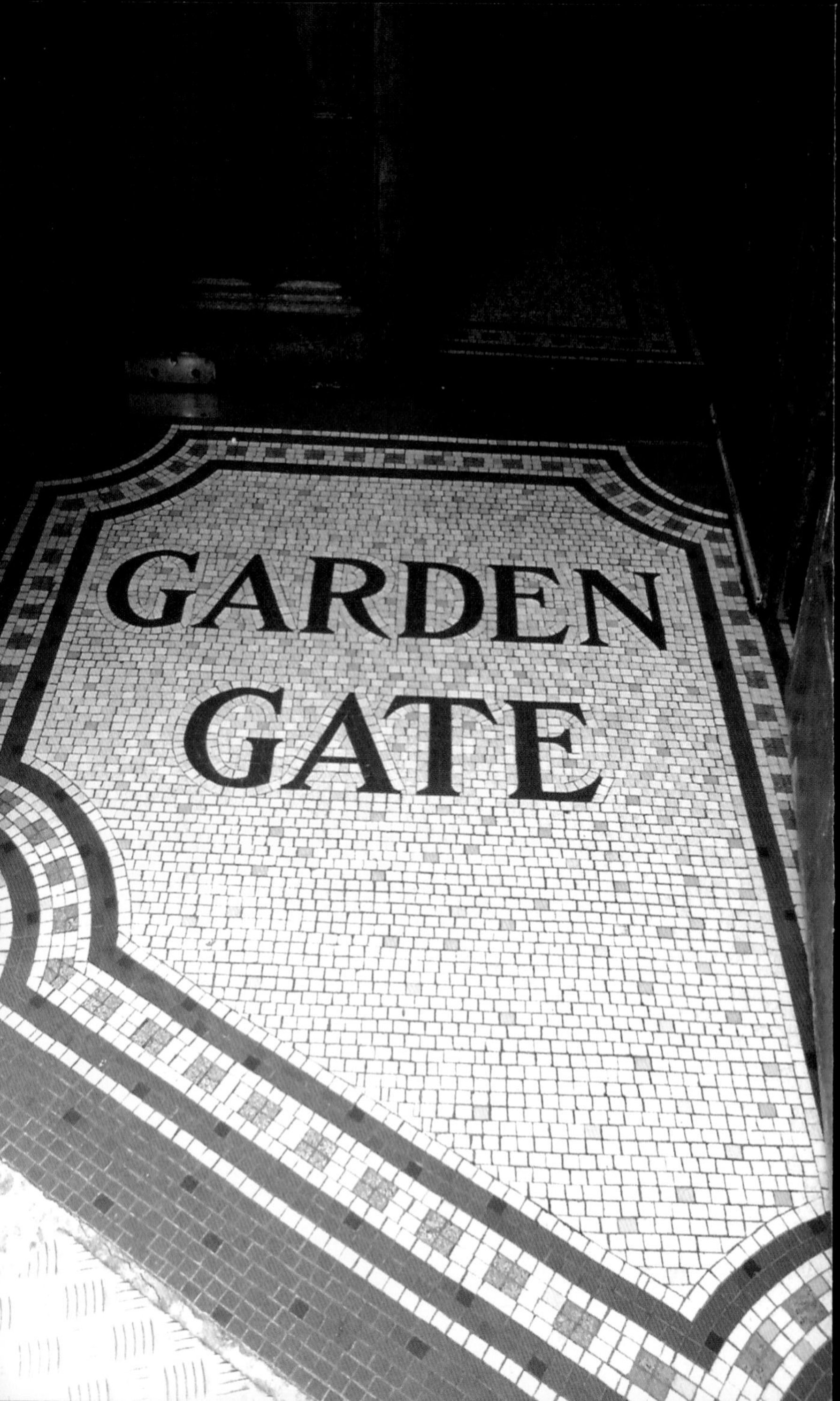
GARDEN
GATE

Leeds Brewery Pub Crawl

Leeds Brewery's pubs are dotted around Leeds city centre and you can do a great crawl in a day. It's the perfect way to get a feel for what Leeds Brewery is about.

From Leeds city centre, begin by taking a short bus journey (check the Metro Yorkshire website for bus times) to the **Garden Gate** in Hunslet. This pub is a Grade II* listed building; a survivor of wars, changing tastes and ownership, and a surprisingly grand place to begin your beer journey – enjoying a Leeds Best in one of Yorkshire's most significant pubs.

Heading back into Leeds, walk up from the bus station, up the Headrow, and pop into the **White Swan**. Nestling under the City Varieties theatre, the White Swan prides itself on post- and pre-show food and beer, with a seasonal menu offering locally-sourced meats and fish. That said, it's not just for theatregoers; expect to find all of Leeds' beer plus guests on offer. Grab yourself a refreshing pint of *Leeds Pale* and take a closer look at those playbills adorning the walls.

Next to Leeds Train Station, the **Brewery Tap** holds Leeds' smaller, experimental brewery, and is the only brewpub in central Leeds. You should be able to taste whatever's brewing that week and – most importantly – *Leodis* lager. Crisp and thirst-quenching with a crisp, grassy finish, you'll be glad you dropped by.

Head under the train station and toward the modern tower of Bridgewater Place, turn right and keep heading along the canal and you'll come to the **Midnight Bell**. Take an old, industrial building (in this case a red-brick mill) and fit it out with clean, modern lines, a mix of old and new furniture, and Leeds beers on the bar, and you have Leeds Brewery's flagship pub. In the summer, the courtyard at the rear is a perfect suntrap to relax with a bottle or two of *Hellfire* with the post-work crowd, or warm up with a rich, nutty *Midnight Bell* in the colder months.

Finally, head back into Leeds and towards the Brewery Wharf. On Dock Street you'll find **Pin**: a little hideaway just up the road from the former Tetley's brewery site. Good food (the burgers are wonderful) and live sports in a convivial, cosy atmosphere are the order of the day here; although do check opening times before visiting.

LITTLE VALLEY
BREWERY
ORGANIC BOTTLE CONDITIONED

RAGG VALE
BITTER

BOLD AND MALTY
ALC 4.2% VOL
BREWED IN YORKSHIRE

Little Valley Brewery
Cragg Vale

Hebden Bridge seems like the perfect place for a free-spirited, cycling-mad Dutch brewer and his partner to set up a brewery. The bohemian, fiercely independent community rooted there mixes creativity and freedom of expression with the austere mills of the surrounding Calder Valley and plain-speaking, honest-to-god Yorkshire pride.

Little Valley's story begins – somewhat fittingly – in Nepal. 'I met Sue in Kathmandu whilst we were both doing our solo bicycle tours, albeit in opposite directions,' recalls Wim van der Spek, head brewer and co-owner. 'I was looking for the world's highest brewery, but I didn't find it. Finding Sue made up for it though!'

Although Wim is the brewer, Sue Cooper is very much the yin to his yang, and a driving force behind Little Valley. If you don't believe in serendipity, Wim's stories will have you adjusting your train of thought.

'Sue had been living and working in Nepal for a couple of years with a community development project in the far north-west of the country. I had just cycled from Holland to Nepal via Tibet, arriving in Tibet over the Karakoram Highway from Pakistan. Sue was just about to start her own cycle journey back to the UK, when we were introduced by a friend. We said goodbye but then I bumped into her again in Rajasthan in India – the rest is history!' he laughs.

Deciding to take the cosmic hint and stick together, the pair came back to Yorkshire to start a business. As far as Wim is concerned, it had to be beer.

Born in Berkel en Rodenrijs – a small town near Rotterdam – Wim's father was a dairy farmer and the family grew up with strong ties to agriculture. This love of nature and co-existing with the land is central to Wim's – and therefore Little Valley's – ethos. 'There is a kind of natural progression into the brewing world. In its simplest form, brewing is very close to nature. I thought about becoming a vet but my love of beer was much stronger.'

Beer was Wim's obsession from an early age. Impressively, the beer club he set up at the age of 18 is still going today. De Gustibus Est Disputandum is still active and has retained almost all of its original members. 'We have our records going back almost 30 years and we still meet up when we can,' Wim explains, clearly proud of the brotherhood of brewing he left behind.

Settled in Yorkshire, Sue and Wim set up the brewery in 2005 after a lengthy period of careful planning. Funds came from their own pockets, as well as a bank loan and a small grant from Calderdale Council. Not long after opening, the brewery received organic certification from the Soil Association, and their *Ginger Pale Ale* carries the Fairtrade mark. Little Valley's brewing water bubbles up from Withens Clough Reservoir. Wim and Sue's philosophy of living closely with the land is certainly evident in the way that Little Valley is run.

Little Valley also supply beer to Suma Wholefoods, the UK's largest independent organic and vegan food wholesaler.

The brewery's location – Turkey Lodge Farm – is as remote as it is serene, sitting at almost 900 feet above sea level, high atop Hebden Bridge and in the gaze of Stoodley Pike, the imposing war memorial. Wim and Sue clearly find a connection with the surrounding landscape – and the community below.

'We wanted to set up the brewery somewhere in the Calder Valley. It's in a beautiful part of the Pennines – with fantastic countryside and lots of little independent communities living side by side. The transport infrastructure makes it good for business too.'

Sue continues: 'So, we found Turkey Lodge Farm – a former

chicken and pig farm, with the retired farmer here converting his agricultural buildings into business units. We think that we have the best views in Yorkshire; we're situated just off England's longest continuous hill climb. It's great for cyclists!'

After setting up the kit and formalising the business, the pair set about concocting their beer range. Although he had brewed in Scotland, Germany and Holland, this was Wim's first professional foray into brewing his beers.

What soon emerged from the fermenting tanks were traditional styles of beer, twisted a little by way of the continent. When you drink a Little Valley beer, you get something slightly different to what you expect, but in an altogether pleasant and refreshing way.

Take *Hebden's Wheat*, for example. Loaded with lemon peel and coriander seeds during the brewing process, it's zesty, fruity and a real change of pace from the usual Pale Ales of Yorkshire; as well as making an excellent liquor to steam seafood in. *Ginger Pale Ale* is just that, but brewed with a light touch in terms of the ginger, providing a warming, spicy/citrus background note rather than bludgeoning you with ginger, which can be incredibly astringent when handled badly.

Withens Pale Ale – something of a flagship beer for Little Valley – is crisply tart and has a certain 'wild' note in the nose, almost akin to wildflowers. Seasonal special *Dutch Courage* is laced with locally picked elderflower – and if you pick up a sweetish, floral note in *Moor Ale*, then you're tasting heather.

Little Valley's first cask beer was sold to the Smithfield Hotel in Manchester, and it was amazingly popular. Word began to spread about the Dutchman and his unique beers from the Calder Valley.

It's testament to Wim's brewing skills that Little Valley brew a singular take on Yorkshire beer, mixing the traditional and the Continental cultures incredibly well. His beers are interesting and unique, and his professional background tells you all you need to know.

'In my late teens I studied for an MSc in Food Science at Wageningen University in Holland,' Wim explains. 'My industrial placement was with the Gulpener Brewery in Holland. Whilst I was there I cultured a wild yeast that was then used for a very old style beer – the *Mestreijcht Aajt*. After qualifying at Wageningen I worked for several years in the food industry in both research and development and quality control for two different companies. I then went to Germany and studied at Doemens World Brew Academy for my Braumeister (Master Brewer) exam.'

Little Valley have treated their fans to interpretations of Continental styles as specials over the years – from *Pontus Hebdanus* (a German-style Alt beer) to *Gustibus*, a Dark Wheat beer. Not only that, but in 2012 Wim took on another project alongside Little Valley, working with the Benedictine community at Ampleforth Abbey to resurrect monastic brewing in Yorkshire.

Hebden Bridge

Determined to do things right, Wim joined Father Wulstan Peterburs on a tour of Trappist breweries in Belgium and the Netherlands, returning with enough anecdotal information to create the recipe for *Ampleforth Double*, a strong beer to make the Benedictines proud. Now widely available, *Ampleforth Double* has a full, peppery nose and strong echoes of fruit cake in the body. It's an interesting beer – one worth seeking out.

Little Valley have grown from that chance encounter in Kathmandu, to one of our region's most fascinating breweries. They've grabbed awards from the Soil Association, Deliciously Yorkshire and countless beer festivals along the way. In an age of cynicism, they have stuck to their guns, produced truly unique beer, and remained true to the dream of working with the land that Wim had all those years ago.

Little Valley Brewery

Turkey Lodge Farm, Cragg Vale, HX7 5TT

www.littlevalleybrewery.co.uk

Hebden's Wheat Abv: 4.5%

Very much in the family of Witbier and Weizen, *Hebden's Wheat* is a gloriously refreshing beer. Naturally hazy, it boasts a spicy aroma of orange pith, coriander and lime which this carries through into the taste. Sweet at first but drying out to a fresh finish, it's perfect for savouring slightly chilled on a Yorkshire summer's afternoon.

Try It with: steamed mussels, lemon meringue pie, gravadlax

Python IPA Abv: 6%

Big, boozy and full-bodied, this Amber IPA has plenty of citrus zest on the nose, with a wet-straw-like note underneath. The body has echoes of hard-boiled sweets with an orange marmalade note running through it. The finish is suitably bitter but warming with alcohol as it dries. A supremely satisfying English IPA.

Try it with: Dundee fruit cake, chicken jalfrezi, goats' cheese

Ginger Pale Ale Abv: 4%

Snappy, crisp and refreshing, *Ginger Pale* successfully balances a wonderfully summery Pale with a hint of fresh, aromatic ginger. Smooth in body, the sip begins with lemon in abundance before that warming, comforting ginger note appears to tingle the tongue long after the sip. Deliciously different.

Try it with: spring onion and pork stir-fry, steamed fish, baked apples with cinnamon

Cheese and Mustard Scones

Cheese and mustard scones are a doddle to make and are a moreish accompaniment to a cheeseboard and a few beers. In a large bowl, sift 200g of self-raising flour with a pinch of salt, and then rub 40g of butter into that, to make breadcrumbs.

Grate in 50g of any cheese you like – although I reckon the stronger, the better! Now, add 100ml of milk, and one heaped tbsp. of wholegrain mustard. Stir it all together and you'll form a dough. Give that a little knead on a floured surface and then cut your scones out. Top with a little grated cheese and some parsley.

Cook on a greased baking tray at 175°C for about 15 minutes, or until a skewer through the middle comes out cleanly. Split and enjoy with butter, cheese, cooked meats – or just a pint of Little Valley's *Moor Ale*!

Magic Rock Brewery
Huddersfield

Richard Burhouse's career in beer started with a plea from a friend. 'I'd bought some local beers for a friend (who wasn't local) to try and he was so impressed, he started asking me where he could get them. I'd drunk so much good beer around the pubs in Huddersfield and around Yorkshire, I knew it was out there – but there weren't many places to buy them other than locally.'

Richard took that cue and set up *My Brewery Tap*, an online beer shop where rabid beer fans could get their fix of beers from Yorkshire and further afield. Much like Tom Fozard's experience of working in beer retail, Richard immersed himself in the eclectic world of beer, marvelling at the choice that was out there and embarking on an education in beer at the same time.

Over the next few months, MBT proved popular – but didn't really provide the level of success that Richard hoped for. He didn't want to give it up. If anything, his experience of MBT confirmed one thing – that he loved working with beer. It would only follow that his plans for a brewery of his own would appear, so that he could put his own bottles in amongst the cornucopia of independent beer available online. 'I needed to do something else – but it's such a great industry, I just had to stay involved.'

And so the process of raising money, finding a space to brew, kit and staff began in earnest. Richard's brother Jonathan joined him and space in the family's warehouse in Huddersfield was cleared out and set aside for the new venture. As for brewing, Richard and Jonathan did take a brewery course, and originally intended to brew – but Richard soon realised that it wasn't his strong suit. Not only that, but he was starting to form an idea of what his beers should taste like – the beers that his increasingly-evolving palate was beginning to enjoy. He couldn't do it alone. He needed someone to help him realise the beers in his head.

'I had tasted so many beers that by the time I started to think of recipes for my own brewery, I knew what I wanted: something more American in style. When I first tried beers from the States, the flavours were so different... *so intense*. That was the flavour I wanted Magic Rock's beers to carry.'

It was around this time that, further south, a local brewer was creating something different in the basement of Sheffield's Hillsborough Hotel. Stuart Ross was brewing under the banner of Crown Brewery and rapidly gaining a reputation for unique, flavourful beers such as *Brooklyn Heights* – an elegant Black IPA – and the popular *Stannington Stout*.

Stuart – who quite possibly possesses the driest sense of humour in Yorkshire – had certainly paid his dues before settling at Crown. His résumé boasts the right names. Starting at Sheffield's Kelham Island Brewery in 2004, he moved to Acorn for a short stint before taking Crown Brewery on – reformulating not only the physical layout of the brewery but also the beer recipes. Limited only by space and equipment, Stuart turned the little microbrewery in the cellar into a real 'one to watch' in a little under three years.

He remembers Richard's first phone call to him. 'He approached me initially for advice on brewery kit. A few months later, he asked me to join him. When Richard explained to me what his vision was – and what beers he wanted to brew – I had to get on board.' As luck would have it, by this time, Stuart was more than ready to move on from Crown.

Richard will happily admit that it wasn't until Stuart joined the team that the brewery began to really live and breathe. 'I was always impressed by how clean and balanced Stuart's beers were. I knew he was right for the job,' he enthuses.

With the expertise in place, Richard, Jonathan and Stuart got their heads together to formulate Magic Rock's beers; a suitably transatlantic mix. 'We simply tried to get a good beer in each of the 'core' flavour ranges, but we really wanted a Red Ale, an IPA and a Double IPA. We just love those kinds of beers!' laughs Richard.

And so the slightly left-field gang of beers that make Magic Rock Brewing what they are were born: *High Wire Pale Ale*, *Cannonball IPA*, *Dark Arts Stout*, *Human Cannonball Double IPA*, *Rapture Red Ale* and *Curious Original Pale Ale*. All punchy in flavour, aroma and attitude, and each one at a strength that means there is something for everyone, despite not outwardly looking like mainstream beers when sitting on the bar.

Stuart is keen to stress another factor that is important to Magic Rock, and one that led to a fairly small core range being launched: consistency. They looked to a favourite Cumbrian brewer as a benchmark for producing consistently excellent cask, kegged and bottled beer. 'Hawkshead's *Red* is one of my favourite beers,' says Stuart. 'We are really keen on getting our beers consistently on form. We don't really want to do too many 'specials' as we really want to become known for our quality, rather than quantity.'

That's not to say they haven't brewed up a few limited edition treats for their customers. *Bearded Lady* Imperial Brown Stout has enjoyed editions aged in both bourbon and tequila barrels, and a Wheat beer (*Clown Juice*) and Black IPA (*Magic 8 Ball*) have proved popular sideshows to Magic Rock's core range.

Magic Rock officially launched in Huddersfield and Leeds in 2011; and, rightly so, their beers received rave reviews from day one. Almost overnight, they became incredibly popular, managing to attract a diverse range of drinkers to their bright, vibrant beers. Everyone, it seemed, loved Magic Rock.

It had been a while since a brewery launched to such anticipation. Richard's knowledge of the beer industry and

From left: Richard Burhouse, Stuart Ross

Stuart's brewing skills were a match made in heaven; the decision to bottle, cask and keg beer straight away inspired; and the fun, modern branding irresistible. Everyone, it seemed, loved Magic Rock.

By not implicitly tying themselves too much to the region in their name they remain slightly exotic, yet retain a cheekily Yorkshire sense of humour. Richard and Stuart are both intensely proud of their Yorkshire heritage, and it's a testament to the richness of that scene that breweries like Magic Rock and Summer Wine – who both produce styles of beer that our region is not particularly known for – are thriving.

It's not surprising that, with Richard's background in retail, that he places a lot of faith in the reach of bottled beer. 'The decision to bottle was simply a desire for people to enjoy our beers at home,' states Richard, matter-of-factly. 'We also love the idea of people eating great food and drinking our beer at home. It's just another area that we wanted to get our beers into from day one.'

Magic Rock's eye-catching pumpclips – featuring a festival of cartoon circus characters and psychedelic freaks – have become incredibly well known on the bars of Yorkshire. The branding was the result of Richard Norgate's graphic design prowess. The designer had worked on an album sleeve by The Arctic Monkeys, and happened to be an acquaintance of Richard.

Norgate's branding proved inspired. The playful detail of the labels completely mirrors the vivacious flavours in Magic Rock's beers.

And the name? A link to the Burhouse family's business, selling gemstones. As we chat, Richard regales us with anecdotes about how the brewery now fills the room in which he spent many a summer sorting gemstones into different shapes and sizes when he was younger. The two businesses still run side-by-side. 'My dad loves how we use this space now,' he smiles. Magic Rocks, indeed.

Magic Rock Brewing

Quarmby Mills, Tanyard Rd, Huddersfield, HD3 4YP

www.magicrockbrewing.com

Curious Abv: 3.9%

This wonderfully fruity Pale Ale is proof that a sessionable Pale doesn't have to be dull. The crisp, zingy Ale is chock-full of grapefruit and lemon notes, with a lip-smackingly dry finish. A perfect thirst-quencher for warmer seasons, you'll find it hard to only drink only one.

Try it with: deep-fried Brie, poached salmon with dill, herbed chicken

Rapture Abv: 4.6%

Magic Rock refer to *Rapture* as a 'Red Hop Ale', and on your first sip, you'll see why. The lush, deep red hue gives away hints of brown sugar and coffee on the sip before finishing with dry orange pith. The dry finish is refreshing and the overall effect is that of a terrifically satisfying pint.

Try it with: smoked sausages, Manchego cheese and cured meat tapas, spiced lamb dishes

Dark Arts Abv: 6%

Stout in both flavour and heart, *Dark Arts* is a big beer indeed. As black as a ringmaster's hat, *Dark Arts* is rich, substantial and carries earthy blackberry notes along with more subtle notes of liquorice and bitter chocolate. The finish is slightly woody with notes of pine and a hint of bonfire smoke.

Try it with: black pudding, blue cheeses, baked vanilla cheesecake

Black Pudding Toasts

For an indulgent brunch, smear fried black pudding onto toasted bread, and top with sliced mushrooms. Any mushroom will do, but I prefer the larger, meatier ones such as ceps or chestnut.

Sauté the mushrooms in butter, a little olive oil, black pepper and a little chopped sage. This is a lovely dish to enjoy with richer beers such as Magic Rock's *Rapture*, or Hambleton's *Nightmare*.

MALLINSONS
BREWING COMPANY

CITRA

HINT OF
GRAPEFRUIT & MANGO

SINGLE HOPPED
ABV 3.9%

LE CONDITI

Mallinsons Brewery
Huddersfield

Tara Mallinson shoves her hand into the silver-foil sack and pulls out a fistful of lime-green, sticky hops, urging me and Elaine Yendall to do the same. We stand there, the three of us, rubbing the resins out of the hop and onto our palms, inhaling deeply. It's like walking through a pine forest.

'Don't they just smell great?' Tara enthuses. 'Cascade are still a favourite of mine', she says, her face lit up with the arrival of a new batch of fresh, fresh hops.

Hops are the magic ingredient that really fire Elaine and Tara's imagination when it comes to dreaming up a Mallinson's beer. Chinook, Citra, Saaz, Willamette, Perle, Simcoe, Sorachi Ace... the list of hop varieties is as endless as it is exotic-sounding – and there aren't many that Mallinsons have not brewed with at some point in their short career so far. So how did two ladies from Huddersfield – a stone-set stronghold of beer in Yorkshire – end up becoming Yorkshire's unofficial torchbearer for hops?

'Well, Tara loves to 'tick' beers, and simply try everything on the bar!' laughs Elaine. 'But when we started (in 2008), the hop harvest was really bad; there was no quality at all. So we picked the best of what we had at the time, and we brewed until we hit upon *Stadium Bitter*'.

A little more in line with 'traditional' tastes, *Stadium Bitter* did well enough to make the drinkers of Yorkshire sit up and take notice of the two new brewsters on the block. But the beer – although it's still brewed – wasn't quite what Tara had in mind when she set out to brew for a living.

Tara recalls how her involvement in a dominoes team introduced her to Mild, Porter and Stout. Before long she was fully immersed in the world of Real Ale. Homebrewing followed, which is where her love affair with hops began. 'I brewed in small batches, and began to understand what the hops actually were and how they affected the taste of the beer'.

'Our core range (*Stadium Bitter*, *Emley Moor Mild*, *Station Best* and *Castle Hill Premium Bitter*) is now only thirty to forty percent of our output – and they normally go a little further afield,' confirms Elaine. The rest of the time is devoted to simply experimenting with hops, sticking steadfastly to the Mallinsons blueprint: paler-than-pale beers, exploding with hop aroma – and a little bit wacky. Hops are where the interest is for both Elaine and Tara; where the real action is – and use of them is what they want to excel at. They haven't brewed a dark beer for months. Brewing this way means a lot of one-off beers, depending on what hop is in good condition at the time.

I ask whether this seemingly chaotic approach is what they were aiming for. 'Part of it is that we don't like being told what to do!' Elaine laughs. 'At the beginning, everyone told us that we absolutely have to have a core range – even fellow brewers – but it simply didn't appeal. Tara loves mixing hops; so now it's just constant experimentation. That's us, as brewers and drinkers.'

Not only that, but the *always-a-new-beer* approach helped them get a foothold in the market. Real Ale attracts 'tickers': drinkers who simply hunt down new beers every week – a market that is incredibly supportive and vital to sales of Real Ale. By brewing new beers constantly, Tara and Elaine ensured that there was always a different offering to keep a pint of Mallinsons in the hands of Yorkshire's most enthusiastic drinkers.

The more I speak to Tara and Elaine, the more I realise that it's not chaotic at all. Both know where their beer is, and make sure it's tested thoroughly. 'We go out three nights a week – drinking our beer as well as others,' says Elaine. 'That's where you get your feedback, immediate and honest.

We can keep an eye on who's keeping our beer right, and we like to get out amongst our customers. It's still a joy for us to walk into a pub and see our beer on the bar.'

Both Elaine and Tara were teachers in a previous life, and, as is often the case, the grind of working in a vocation you no longer care for wore them both down. 'We'd had a really bad week,' Elaine recalls. 'And we were sat having a beer, moaning to each other. I finally asked Tara what her perfect job would be. She said it was to have our own brewery.'

So brewing it had to be. After years of hard saving, the pair finally took the plunge. The brewhouse was a former garage, and the kit custom-made for them.

Life wasn't easy in the beginning. Tara left her job first, whilst Elaine carried on working, ensuring some income was flowing inwards. 'I could brew twice a week, wash, sterilize the kit, and sell the beer, on my own. That was it. I couldn't physically do any more,' remembers Tara. Eventually Elaine joined Tara and the couple worked full-time, seven days a week.

Launched without fanfare, Mallinsons' first beers sold well, and they began to make a name for themselves in and around Huddersfield. The 'slow burn' approach suited them, using only minimal marketing and relying on word of mouth to get their beers into the pubs of Yorkshire.

Initially, the forays into single-hopped beers were named, somewhat cheekily, 'Now That's What I Call Hops', with each volume representing a hop. This evolved into their current range, in which each beer is named after the hop involved.

'The re-brand came out because we wanted to look a bit more grown-up, and look a little better on the bar,' smiles Tara, flicking through a handful of the pumpclips. Elaine reveals another community link with the new-look clips. 'One of our friends is a lecturer in design at Huddersfield University, and she asked us whether we'd like to collaborate on a project for the students. We asked for some new labels for

From left: Elaine Yendall, Tara Mallinson

our single-hopped range, and these designs,' she adds, holding up a new *Saaz* clip, 'were the winning design. We picked the winning design, but we were so impressed that we kept them on.'

Mallinsons beers can now be found from Lancashire to London and they have permanent pumps in Huddersfield – the Sportsman being the first. The Star – which is now next door to Mallinsons new brewhouse – also take a massive amount of beer. Such is the popularity of Mallinsons that they are practically a house brand for many of Huddersfield's fine pubs.

All of their bottled beers are bottle-conditioned (a process whereby an extra fermentation takes place in the bottle) and, impressively, they do it themselves with the help of a friend in the brewery's office. The bottles are even labelled by hand, too.

'We looked into contract bottling, but we didn't want to filter our beer. We feel it takes too much out of the beer's flavour,' says Tara.

Mallinsons' overt use of hops is now their niche. Many breweries across the UK brew single-hop beers to celebrate the hop itself or to experiment with a new, unknown variety; but Mallinsons make celebration of the hop a cornerstone of their brewery. Simply put, it's *who they are*. Tara and Elaine have built Mallinsons from a struggling start-up – a new brewery in a crowded marketplace – into a brewery with a cult following. Their fans follow the myriad of sunny Pale Ales across the region, and the Mallinsons name is now synonymous with brewing in Huddersfield.

Mallinsons moved into new premises during 2012, which will give them the scope to allow tours and set up a brewery shop where you can indulge your hop addiction to the full. Huddersfield, you have been warned.

MALLINSONS BREWING COMPANY

SAAZ

LIGHT AND GENTLE
BITTERNESS

SINGLE HOPPED
ABV 4.1%

CONDITIONED

MALLINSONS BREWING COMPANY

AMARILLO

PALE GOLD AND BITTER
ORANGE

SINGLE HOPPED
BV 4.3%

MALLINSONS BREWING COMPANY

MOTUEKA

BLONDE AND FRUITY

SINGLE HOPPED
ABV 4.2%

BOTTLE CONDITIONED

Mallinsons Brewery

Unit 1, Waterhouse Mill, 65-71 Lockwood Road,
Huddersfield, HD1 3QU

www.drinkmallinsons.co.uk

Danger: Hops! Abv: 5%

Straw-pale, with a pungent aroma of fresh mango and pineapple. *Danger: Hops* follows the Mallinsons blueprint – light, a touch of grainy cereal in the body and a long, lip-puckeringly dry finish of lemon peel and pink grapefruit.

Try it with: lemon sorbet, aged Cheddar, sweet and sour chicken

Stadium Bitter Abv: 3.8%

This gold-hued Ale is Mallinsons' take on the 'classic' Yorkshire bitter. With an aroma that suggests wildflowers and a faint lick of honey, and a crisp, tart finish, it's a refreshing beer – and certainly bitter!

Try it with: beer-battered fish, rabbit stew, scallops wrapped in Parma ham

Centennial Abv: 3.9%

One of Mallinsons' best-selling single-hopped beers. Pale malts provide the backdrop to a beer that's got heaps of pine-needle and earthy spice notes in the nose and a typically long, drying finish that's helped along with waves of grapefruit. A superbly flavourful beer for the strength.

Try it with: Jamaican jerk pork, seafood salad, asparagus with hollandaise sauce and poached egg

MALLINSON

BREWING COMPANY

SORACHE ACE

PALE BITTER
AROMATIC
LEMONGRASS

SINGLE HOPPED
ABV 3.9%

BOTTLE CONDITIONED

Tasty Taster

Beer-Battered Mussels

Mussels work really well as a beer snack wrapped in crisp beer batter. Beer batter couldn't be easier. Just mix plain flour with enough beer to make a batter that's about the consistency of double cream. Add a little salt and a twist of ground black pepper, and it's done.

Dip each mussel in the batter and deep-fry in hot oil.

When browned take out and drain on absorbent paper. Douse liberally in salt, lemon and – if you fancy – cayenne pepper for a little heat. They are delicious with pale, bitter Ales like the ones Mallinsons brew.

Revolutions Brewing Co
Castleford

When you meet Andy Helm and Mark Seaman – collectively known as Revolutions Brewing – it's entirely normal to spend the first part of your conversation talking about music. Eventually, you'll get round to beer, but make no mistake, music is the inspiration behind the beers that this Castleford-based partnership produce.

Andy had been one of Yorkshire's many keen homebrewers – and had even taken the step of completing a course at Brewlab, Sunderland's hands-on brewing business course. 'For me, going to Brewlab was more a question of learning about the business side of things – how much would it cost me to set up, that sort of thing,' he says.

Meanwhile, Mark's course in life had led him to Bahrain as a quality control consultant. Upon arriving back in the country after considerable time in the Middle East, he found himself at a crossroads in life. 'When I returned, I realised I was virtually unemployable!' he laughs. 'In the back of my mind, I was wondering what sort of business I could get involved in to see me through the next phase of my life.'

In early 2009, the pair's paths crossed through a mutual friend at a business seminar, and they immediately found they had much in common. Cricket, beer and music became the topic of conversation, and they stayed in touch thereafter. Many shared drinking sessions, many albums listened to, and many conversations led to the notion of setting up a brewery. As Mark puts it, starting a brewery was 'an idea that just wouldn't go away.' After a typically low-key meeting in the Shoulder of Mutton in Castleford, the pair decided to go for it.

Even then, the theme of musically-themed beers pushed itself to the fore of Andy and Mark's vision; and it was even the branding of Revolutions Brewing – rather than the recipes for the beers – which brought things to life for Andy. 'The prospect of the niche that we could inhabit was really exciting,' he says.

Mark elaborates: 'We'd kicked around a few ideas – all music-related – but then Andy came up with the idea of using record speeds as 'families': the 33's, the 45's the 78's, and so on.'

The idea was astoundingly simple, yet entirely astute: brew a set of beers with alcohol volumes that match the speeds of vinyl records (4.5% abv, for example). 'Nobody else was doing that, and it just resonated. That was the lightbulb moment,' smiles Mark.

Revolutions Brewery in Castleford is a clean, modern brewplant in an industrial unit – as often is the case these days. It was essentially custom-built, and that meant a long wait before they could start to realise their dream. Mark and Andy were keen to get started, and in early 2010 they decided to get the show on the road with a spot of cuckoo brewing – brewing at other people's breweries.

The concept of 'Cuckoo Brewing' is simple and gaining in popularity: find an accommodating brewer, arrange to brew on their kit on a part-time basis, and get your beers on the market without the overheads associated with owning a full-time business. Richard Billington at Brass Monkey Brewery (Sowerby Bridge) offered to help, and Andy and Mark set out bringing their beers to life.

Operating in this way not only gave the friends chance to get hands-on experience and test their own skills in brewing, but also to make tentative steps in the market. Even when the first prototype Revolutions beers were hitting the bars of Castleford, York and Leeds, they truly looked unlike anything out there. Not only that, but there was another uncommon aspect to them: in a region known for floral, hoppy Pale Ales, Revolutions' beers were all Dark.

From left: Andrew Helm, Mark Seaman

'We started out only brewing Dark Ales simply because we like to drink them!' laughs Andy. 'Not only that, but it's a talking point. We felt that we didn't want to be all things to all people, and we worked out what we were good at – and it was what our new customers seemed to want,' says Andy. Mark backs him up. 'We weren't going to brew another version of Timothy Taylor's *Landlord*. Taylor's do that well enough. We wanted to make something a little more unique – without being too radical.'

The notion was spot on. It seems odd to launch a brewery with a dark style of beer but *Clash London Porter* was wildly popular, and remains the foundation that the Revolutions house is built on. The rich, smoky Porter has a legion of fans, and its name alone provides more than enough interest. 'Associating your beer with bands gives people another aspect to latch onto as well, rather than just the beer,' adds Andy.

As the duo found their feet in the brewhouse, a sweet, light Brown Ale (or, as they put it, "Braun" ale) by the name of *Kraftwerk* was introduced. *Devolution Amber Ale* and *Ravenscroft Pale Ale* joined the permanent roster not long after that. A popular seasonal – *Beat Red* (a full-bodied, malty Ale with a devilishly scarlet hue) – had its popularity rewarded with a place in the core range. '*Beat* was originally called *The Scream*,' recalls Mark. 'It was received really well and we liked it, so it became permanent.'

Andy is more than aware that the initial decision to brew darker Ales gave them a unique personality in the early days. 'There's still nothing quite like the *Kraftwerk* out there, we think,' says Andy. 'Brown Ales weren't really on people's radar at the time,' he adds. I'd have to agree – despite being a classic northern English style.

Revolutions' main beers are all mid-strength; perfect for session drinking, but retain such malt body that they have a dimension to them often missing from identikit Pale Ale merchants. They have depth and balance – and are deeply rewarding as a result. Not only that, but Mark and Andy are trying to use as many English hops as they can in their beers.

Alongside the regular range, a small army of one-off beers with names inspired by classic albums have graced the bars of Yorkshire; always providing a talking point, a point of reference to those unfamiliar with Revolutions' beer.

In the last year, another aspect of the Revolutions blueprint has started to emerge: direct collaboration with Yorkshire's fertile grass-roots music scene. Not only were Mark and Andy working to get their beers into pubs, but live music venues such as the legendary Brudenell Social Club in Leeds were approached. Now, they have a semi-permanent pump there and that couldn't please Mark and Andy enough.

In addition, Revolutions turned to supporting local bands, to provide a unique form of collaboration. So far, they've worked with a number of young bands from Yorkshire, getting them into the brewery for a day and producing a one-off beer that can then be enjoyed at album launches and even taken on tour. Revolutions have also produced one-off brews for International Record Store Day and the 25th birthday of Leeds' legendary independent record shop, Jumbo.

'It's a win-win – it's fun, enjoyable, and we can both cross-pollinate fans of the bands and fans of the beer and work together.' Mark and Andy are clearly proud of supporting music in their own way.

It also puts their beers into the hands of a socially-aware, somewhat younger group of people who genuinely want to taste a unique, locally-produced beer.

'There's a changing demographic with Real Ale or Craft Beer, or whatever you want to call it,' says Andy. 'When we started out planning our brand image, some people said that the younger crowd won't 'get it'. Yes, they may download and buy CDs, but they still love vinyl; and young bands still produce it, too. Real Ale is the same. There are plenty of people that drink our beers – and Real Ale in general – that are like-minded, enthusiastic and young. Getting our beers into places other than traditional pubs drives that along.'

In early 2012 Revolutions Brewing took the 'Meet the Brewer' concept one step further, holding music events. The idea is simple: find a supportive pub, take over the bar with your beer, and put on some live music. So far, there have been *Love Music: Love Beer* nights in York, Sheffield and Leeds.

'The benefit of having your own pub is that you can sell people your own beer in the perfect setting. But we can't do that – so we put on our own nights instead. We've got a handful of venues that we can work with, and will continue to do so. We make sure there is plenty of our beer on the bar, we play good music, and people can understand what we are really about,' Mark says.

Revolutions Brewing Co will keep marching to the beat of their own drum, expanding as they go and spreading their mantra – Love Music: Love Beer – across the land. Watch out for them in a venue near you soon.

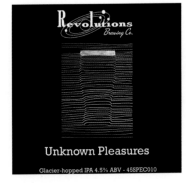

Ravenscroft
Pale Ale
Revolutions
Brewing Co.
4·5
% ABV
The Revolutions Brewing Company Ltd
Yorkshire
CLASH
LONDON PORT
Revolutions
Brewing Co.
4·5
% ABV
The Revolutions Brewing Company Ltd
Yorkshire
Revolutions
Brewing Co.
4·5
% ABV
The Revolutions Brewing Company Ltd
Revolutions
Brewing Co.
4·5
% ABV
The Revolutions Brewing Company Ltd

Revolutions Brewing Co.

Whitwood Enterprise Park, Castleford, WF10 5PX

www.revolutionsbrewing.co.uk

Kraftwerk Braun Ale Abv: 4.5%

Reviving the Brown Ale genre in Germanic tones, Revolutions 'Braun' Ale is a robust, nutty pint with an emphasis on rich, biscuit malt and a crisp, clean finish with echoes of ginger biscuit. A truly Northern session beer.

Try it with: roasted pork sandwiches, pork pie and pickles, pizza

Manifesto Strong Stout Abv: 6.0%

Push through that thick, silky head and you've got a real winter warmer on your hands. Milk chocolate and digestive-biscuit-esque cereals lurk in the aroma, and the body is smooth and deep in flavour, with raisin and espresso coffee coming to the fore. The finish is almost unexpectedly fruity, laden with earthy blackberry and plum notes.

Try it with: creme caramel, bean chilli, beef burritos

Clash London Porter Abv: 4.5%

Full of body, *Clash London Porter* is a rewarding, rich beer that fans of the style will fall in love with. Mocha and roasted coffee bean notes arrive on the palate first, followed by swirls of sweet woodsmoke and a hint of raisin. The finish is bittersweet and pleasingly dry.

Try it with: prawn cocktail, Christmas pudding, blue cheese tarts

Red Onion Tart

Ready-made puff pastry sheets make an excellent base for off-the-cuff tarts. To make a tasty starter or veggie main course, simply sweat three large, sliced red onions in a heavy-bottomed pan in butter and a little oil. When they start to turn translucent, stir in about 25g of brown sugar.

Stir, and let that reduce down. Soon you'll have sweet, sticky caramelised onion. Spread the onion over a sheet of pastry – leaving room at the edges – and lay slices of goats' cheese on top. Bake in a hot oven for about 25 minutes or until the edges are golden. This tart is wonderful accompanied by darker, maltier beers such as Revolutions' *Beat Red* or Rudgate's smoky *Ruby Mild*.

WILD
MULE

ROOSTERS
FREE RANGE BEERS FROM YORKSHIRE

EST. 1993

Rooster's Brewing Co
Knaresborough

In 2001, Ol Fozard – who was just starting out in brewing – heard that Rooster's Brewing Co was relocating to Knaresborough from Harrogate. Sensing an opportunity, the young lad wrote to Sean Franklin, offering his services. A response soon arrived: a polite explanation that no jobs were available. Nevertheless, in a typically gracious act, Sean offered to meet the young brewer for a beer and a chat. Ol remembers it well.

'We met for a pint in Harrogate. We had a good chat, and he explained what I could do to learn more about the art of brewing and help me understand how far I wanted to go in the industry. I really took his advice on board.'

As Ol recounts this story, you can tell that it's a truly life-changing moment for him. Regardless of the strange twist of fate that transpired ten years later, Sean Franklin remained a mentor to the fledgling brewer through the years.

If there's one modern Yorkshire brewer that needs no introduction, it's Sean Franklin. Setting up Rooster's Brewing Co in the early nineties, he built the brewery from scratch, finding his voice early on and setting the standard for aromatic Pale Ales that showcased hops: super-pale, elegantly fruity beers that stood out like beacons in a sea of fudgy Best Bitters and smoky Milds. Beers like *Yankee* and *YPA* (Yorkshire Pale Ale) garnered awards worldwide. A modest man, Sean – alongside his wife, Alison – continued to quietly revolutionise Pale Ale from his quiet corner of Knaresborough.

So, when Sean and Alison made the decision to retire in

2011, drinkers in Yorkshire were concerned. Rightly so. To lose Rooster's would be a massive blow – the brewery deserved more than to simply be a footnote in the region's independent brewing history. Simply put, the brewery deserved to live on.

Luckily, Ian Fozard – then MD of Market Town Taverns – felt the same way. A long-time friend of the Franklins and prominent CAMRA member, Fozard bought the business, with the intention of his two sons, Ol and Tom, running Rooster's.

Make no mistake, this was no simple flight of fancy by a man with means. If there's one thing that the Fozards know, it's beer. The siblings are twins; and after you've spent a little time with them, you realise that a lot of clichés about twins ring true. Both possess a wicked sense of humour and a shared love of football – although Tom follows Leeds United while Ol is a servant of Sheffield Wednesday. When it comes to talking beer, both often finish each other's sentences and talk very much in a united front. Both have clearly made their choice in life to brew beer – although approaching Ale from very different angles.

'I went on a brewery tour of Black Sheep when I was a teenager, and decided there and then that this was what I wanted to do,' smiles Ol, obviously fond of the memory.

College then beckoned, and for Ol this was largely fuelled by such local Ales as Timothy Taylor's iconic *Landlord*, which, by his own admission, 'was the first beer I really, really liked'. College completed, a visit to the job centre served up the next little twist of fate: a vacancy in a brewery. That brewery was Harrogate's Daleside Brewery, which became Ol's place of work for the next four years.

Those years rolled by, and when Skipton's Copper Dragon announced an expansion, Ol once again saw an opportunity. He left Daleside to work alongside Gordon Wilkinson at Copper Dragon – relocating in the process – and got stuck

From left:
Ol Fozard,
Tom Fozard
(Photo courtesy
of Tom Bishop)

(Photos courtesy of Tom Bishop)

in brewing such well-known beers as *Golden Pippin* and *Black Gold*.

Tom had previously worked in publishing after leaving university, but redundancies ended that line of work. After a stint working at The Old Bell pub in Harrogate, Tom started work for Beer-Ritz, Headingley's bottled beer haven. Tom discovered a whole new world of beers from around the world, and it was these constant discoveries that inspired his brother.

'Tom introduced me to so many beers that I'd never heard of,' laughs Ol. 'Not only that, but these new flavours and styles gave me a renewed desire to brew.'

It followed that Tom began to brew at home – initially to save a little money – recreating the beers that he was enjoying week in, week out. This interest in the nuts-and-bolts of brewing any style he might fancy led to grander plans, and, before long, Tom was already formulating nascent plans for a brewery of his own when the Rooster's sale came about.

Surprisingly, the purchase of Rooster's by the Fozards was as much a surprise to the boys as Sean's decision to retire was. When Ian and his sons discussed whether taking on Rooster's was a feasible plan, it wasn't a decision taken lightly. 'When the idea was put to us', explains Tom, 'we really had to think about it. It wasn't as easy a decision as you may think. All three of us are quite opinionated people and we had to understand whether we could work together. It's not just a case of "Here's some money, go and play at running a brewery."'

Likewise, the reputation of the brewery in question played a part in the Fozard's trepidation too. Despite the fear of the unknown, Tom realised that the opportunity was plain to see, not only in the beer but in the whole Rooster's ethos.

'We all loved the beers. We all loved the branding – that iconic rooster. The whole package was perfect. For me, I had to understand how I could not only respect that but take it forward,' says Tom.

Much of the latter part of 2011 was spent at the brewery shadowing Sean and Alison, not only in brewing, but in *The Way of the Rooster*. This smooth transition was something that everyone involved insisted on, being aware of the cult following that the brewery has. The handover had to be smooth – and as brewers, being shown the ropes and taught daily by Sean Franklin was an education that money can't buy, as far as Ol is concerned.

'Working with Sean was fantastic. Previously I had essentially been a production brewer, making someone else's beers to their standards and tastes – no matter how high those standards are. To be involved from day one in terms of recipe and flavour was wonderful. Tom and I learned constantly about things like off-flavours, colour and what is desirable in a beer and what isn't,' enthuses Ol.

As well as taking in Sean's considerably expert knowledge, that Rooster's ethos began to soak in, too.

'Sean gave me so much encouragement to be bold: to do what I want to do and not look at or worry about anybody else. *Make the beer you want to make*. If it turns out great then well done – if not, then try again. That's what it's all about.'

Now, alongside a small, long-serving team of staff, Tom and Ol are standing on their own two feet, with Ol taking the mantle of head brewer. So, what makes a Rooster's beer?

'The Rooster's style is clean and hop-forward – but well-balanced,' states Ol without hesitation. This is qualified further by Tom: 'Just because a beer is 'hop-forward' it can still remain delicate. Our beers are brewed in such a way that we make sure that the malt background always remains sympathetic to the hop. The beers have to be drinkable. That's what defines our beers.'

The Fozard twins are acutely aware of the history of the

brewery and the reverence in which Rooster's is held – not only in the county, but in the world. The core range of *Yankee* and *Wild Mule* will continue to be brewed along with *YPA*; not just because of that history, but because they are modern classics.

Outlaw Brewing (the brewery's arm for creating more experimental brews) has also been reborn to serve up something for the more adventurous drinker – the first brew, an IPA dosed with jasmine green tea, brewed in collaboration with with beer writer, Melissa Cole, and Taylor's of Harrogate.

Tom and Ol will continue on their own upward trajectory of creating beers the best way they know how: aromatic, elegantly refreshing, and, above all, balanced in flavour. That, after all, is the Rooster's way.

BREWED IN COLLABORATION WITH MELISSA COLE & TAYLORS OF HARROGATE

Roosters Brewing Co

Unit 3, Grimbald Park, Knaresborough HG5 8LJ

www.roosters.co.uk

Wild Mule Abv: 3.9%

This showcase in hops is perfectly representative of Rooster's ethos: light, fresh and loaded with an amazing aroma of grapefruit, lemon, lime and orange. Super-pale in colour with high, drying bitterness.

Try it with: Key lime pie, frutti di mare, grilled monkfish

Yankee Abv: 4.3%

Pale gold in hue, *Yankee* is the beer that made Rooster's name. Softly bitter, with a firm biscuit-malt backbone, the finish is typically clean and tropical fruit-loaded with a slightly herbal aftertaste. A fragrant take on the typical Pale 'Yorkshire Bitter'.

Try it with: chicken pie, Caprese salad, paella

YPA (Yorkshire Pale Ale) Abv: 4.3%

Slightly darker than *Yankee*, *YPA* is, as the name suggests, another variant on the typical Rooster's session Ale. A body of bready malt is washed away by a long, citrusy finish, and topped off with another fruit-bowl aroma so typical of Rooster's beers.

Try it with: roast Chinese-style pork, honey and mustard sausages, Bakewell tart

Calamari

Possibly my favourite match for fragrant, light Pales, such as the ones Rooster's brew, is simple calamari. I find that buying fresh, whole squid – but freeze it until you need it – actually tenderises it.

So, defrost your squid, clean it, and slice the body into rings. Rinse with cold water, and then pat dry. On a large plate, mix plain flour with lemon zest, black pepper and a little paprika. All you need to do then is dredge the calamari through your seasoned flour, and fry in batches in hot oil.

Serve with plenty of lemon, sea salt, and cold beer. Wonderful.

Market Town Taverns

MTT are a small chain of pubs dotted around Yorkshire – from Northallerton to Leeds – that offer a huge selection of cask beers from Yorkshire. Having an excellent reputation for food, dog-friendly and without TV screens or music, you can be sure of a warm welcome, locally-sourced food and that all-important well-kept pint of Yorkshire beer. Check their website for bar and pub locations.

Saltaire Brewery
Shipley

From the outside, Saltaire Brewery isn't much to look at. The building sits in an industrial estate, familiar detritus from the creation of beer littering the yard: barrels, pallets, and the obligatory liveried brewery van being loaded with steel casks.

However, inside sits one of the most charming breweries you'll find in Yorkshire. The gleaming steel brewery is crammed into the lower floor, towering above imperiously as you walk through. Steps up to a mezzanine reveal a malt store and bar area. Fermentation tanks stand proudly behind plates of glass like exhibits in a museum. Colourful signs describe the brewing process, and the whole brewery has the feel of a split-level *Wacky Warehouse* for discerning adults.

Tony Gartland, the man behind Saltaire Brewery, smiles warmly when I comment how lovely the whole building is. 'It's a converted Victorian power station. It used to burn refuse from Shipley and Saltaire, which would then power the turbines and send power to the tram sheds in Saltaire roundabout. After the war, it sent power to the grid.'

Tony spent twenty years in corporate law before deciding that, after retirement, there was still some gas in the tank. A keen homebrewer, he took the lauded Brewlab course in Sunderland in 2004 before helping out at Darwin, Brewlab's microbrewery.

With the help of Derek Todd (who was also at Darwin) the pair decided to break off and set up their own brewery, with Salt's Mill in Saltaire being the first choice of location. After a period of discussion, however, it became clear that the commercial venture would not fit with the heritage of Salt's Mill. One afternoon shortly after, Tony took a bike ride along the canal, and spotted the current site sitting idle.

It's apt, then, that the site now produces beer that slakes much of Yorkshire's thirst; particularly Saltaire's superlative *Blonde*. 'It accounts for about 60% of our output at the moment!' Tony adds. This crisp, straw-hued beer is by far their biggest seller, and it's difficult to drink socially in these parts without bumping into it.

'In the beginning we set out to make Pale Ales with a single varietal hop,' Tony recalls, listing the first set of beers that emerged from the brewery in 2005. 'We had *Fuggles*, *Goldings* and *Challenger*. *Fuggles* was a good beer but people didn't seem to get the name! *Challenger* is still about, but *Blonde* has since taken over *Goldings*' place.'

The business grew with the help of Tony's neighbour, Paul Simpson. Paul had a background in commercial sales (he's now at Aspall Cider) and he worked at getting Saltaire's beers into pubs whilst Tony and Derek manned the brewhouse, finding their feet with their new kit. Paul left the team in 2008 to pursue his own career.

'Those first beers turned out well, but the kit was tricky to brew with initially. It took us a while to understand how it worked, and how we could achieve balance in the beer.' Tony's account of wrestling with the snarling kettle, spitting scalding steam and beer everywhere, certainly fits the 'satanic mills' feel of the brewery.

'Once we got our heads around the process, *Cascade Pale Ale* (featuring the superlative American hop with a fresh, grapefruit-led edge) was our first real commercial hit,' says Tony. Today, Saltaire's *Cascade* remains massively popular, and is a multiple award winner.

Despite Tony's deft hand with Pale Ales, there's another string to Saltaire's bow. When you speak to Tony about food, you can sense Tony's mind shift gear. He's a man who loves cooking, flavours and experimenting. We discuss this at length – for example, how Wheat Beer is a more versatile match for spiced foods than Lager or Pale Ale – and this love of experimentation in the kitchen comes through in Saltaire's use of flavouring, which has produced such beers as *Hazelnut Coffee Porter*, *Raspberry Cascade* and *Elderflower Blonde*.

'Initially we started flavouring beers as we had the resource to split a batch of Pale Ale down and flavour them individually. A batch of *Blonde*, for example, would become three other beers.'

As a brewer, this scope to experiment is where the creative mind comes to the fore. It was a relief to the team as they found that the flavoured beers were popular, too. As someone who doesn't particularly choose flavoured beers, I can certainly vouch for Saltaire's being surprisingly drinkable; always balanced and genuinely interesting. *Hazelnut Coffee Porter* is a real treat; like Toblerone in a glass.

Testament to this is the sheer success of *Triple Chocoholic*, a Stout with a Bournville-esque hit of chocolate swirling around in the glass. Importantly, the beers have no air of novelty and are produced with the same care as Saltaire's core range.

'I had tried loads of chocolate beers – both here and abroad – but they were always a little sickly and cloying,' grimaces Tony. 'But I really wanted to brew a Chocolate Stout.' The inspiration, in the end, was Young's famous *Double Chocolate Stout*. 'That beer – along with the likes of Dark Star's *Espresso Stout* – was inspiration for our beer. We have to brew the base beer slightly differently, and we add commercial syrups and cocoa for both *Triple Chocolate* and *Hazelnut Coffee Porter*.'

Tony continues to reel off postcard-like recollections of flavour inspirations. 'We were walking down Oxford Street in London, doing some Christmas shopping, and nipped into Starbucks for a coffee. I had hazelnut syrup in mine, and thought it was wonderful. So, once back home, we added coffee beans to our base Porter in the boil, added syrup later,

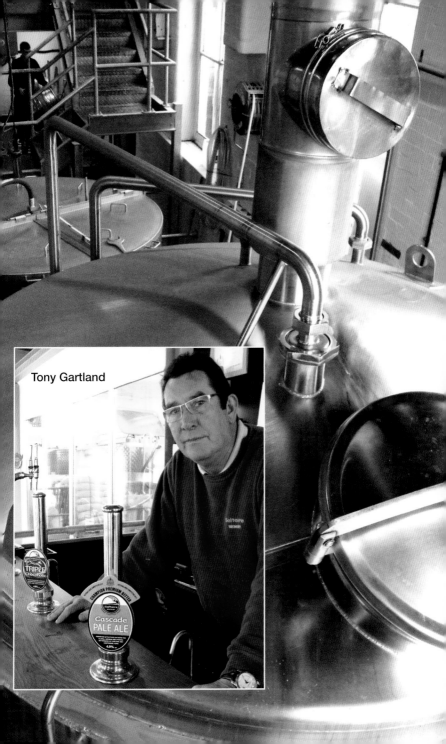

Tony Gartland

and *hey presto! Hazelnut Coffee Porter* was born.'

It's clear that Tony looks to food for inspiration for Saltaire's more esoteric beers. The malt store at the brewery has the largest variety of malt that I've seen: Chocolate, Rye and Oat malts all nestle happily alongside the base Maris Otter malt that makes up so much of the beer you drink today. In fact, the malt store is more like a larder than a functional, run-of-the-mill malt store.

There's another area of beer that Tony draws inspiration from: homebrewing. Homebrewing is enjoying something of a renaissance at the moment, and it's shedding its somewhat dated image of men in sheds emptying packets of dried malt into buckets and creating super-strength – but largely undrinkable – beer.

Tony and his team have been hugely supportive to the homebrewing scene in Yorkshire, hosting awards ceremonies and keeping one eye on what the would-be brewers out there are actually creating.

'I'm a massive fan of homebrewing groups both in the UK and the US, and a member of all the groups. It's a great source of inspiration. You can see where trends are going. We created our *Black IPA* as a reaction to the trend that we could see coming a mile off.' As he speaks, you can genuinely feel the admiration that he has for these garage brewers, pushing boundaries that commercial brewers, tied to orders and cashflow, can only dream of. Tony hints at a possible pilot plant appearing soon in order to satisfy his – and his team's – inquisitive minds.

Saltaire also pioneered the Beer Club. Theirs is the one that everyone else looks up to, and the brewery is the perfect place for it. The inspiration for the Beer Club, however, was something a little more than simply 'getting punters through the door'.

'Our strapline has always been "Mission to Inform",' he states, proudly. 'We have the recipes for our beers on the label, and we're very open in letting people know how we do things. The visitors' centre came from the Mansfield Brewery, and we've hosted school trips and groups like that in the past. It's been popular from day one. Having the bar and letting people into the brewery was something we wanted to do since the start.'

Beer Club emerged in 2008, a monthly event – so as not to affect local trade too much or become too much of a permanent fixture – that remains ridiculously popular to this day. Saltaire also go that extra mile in sourcing guest Ales (such as those brewed by Bristol's Dark Star and Otley, from Pontypridd) to sit alongside their own brews, and also host seasonal beer festivals.

Saltaire's beers are amongst the most popular in the region. They have award-winners, cult favourites and beers for every occasion in their stable. From that bubbling, steaming brewery set in brick and steel emerge some of the region's most individual beers. Seek them out and you'll find something ultimately rewarding – whichever beer you choose.

What is a Beer Society?

Beer Societies or (Beer Clubs) are a great way to really get to know a brewery. Normally held monthly throughout the warmer months, the brewery doors will be flung open for you to enjoy beer directly from the brewery itself, chat to the brewers and enjoy some food and entertainment. Both Ilkley and Saltaire Breweries run popular (and very busy!) ones, and there are even sometimes chances to try prototype beers before they are available to the general public. All are welcome, so keep an eye out for ones in your area and get involved!

CASCADE PALE ALE

~

AMERICAN STYLE PALE ALE WITH
THE FLORAL AROMAS AND STRONG
BITTERNESS OF CASCADE AND
CENTENNIAL HOPS.

4.8% ABV

SALTAIRE BLONDE

~

STRAW COLOURED LIGHT ALE WITH
SOFT MALT FLAVOURS, DELICATELY
HOPPED WITH CZECH AND
GERMAN HOP VARIETIES.

4% ABV

RASPBERRY BLONDE

~

A REFRESHING BLONDE ALE
DELICATELY INFUSED WITH
RASPBERRY FLAVOURS.

4% ABV

Saltaire Brewery

County Works, Dockfield Road, Shipley, BD17 7AR

www.saltairebrewery.co.uk

Cascade Pale Ale Abv: 4.8%

Cascade Pale Ale does what it says on the pumpclip; a showcase for the famous Cascade hop. Pale gold in hue, the aroma is full of subtle pine needle and lemon-rind. The body of the beer is light with whispers of cereal, but a spritz of pithy, bitter grapefruit at the end leads to a crisp finish.

Try it with: spit-roasted chicken, lemon sole, trio of melon with watercress

Blonde Abv: 4%

Saltaire's biggest seller and it's easy to see why. A near-perfect session Ale with continental aspirations, you've got Lager-esque bready taste and aroma to both the nose and body, which is topped off with a soft, sweet finish with just a hint of lemon to freshen things up.

Try it with: salted pretzels or rustic bread, honey-glazed gammon, goats' cheese tart

Hazelnut Coffee Porter Abv: 4.6%

Toblerone in a glass; smooth, rich and undeniably sweet. The enticing aroma of hazelnut and freshly-pressed espresso continues into the body where it meets milk chocolate. The beer finishes sweet with residual nuttiness carrying on for what seems like an age. A warming, comforting treat, especially when enjoyed when taking refuge from autumnal weather.

Try it with: chocolate mousse, almond biscuits, Yorkshire parkin

Chocolate Truffles

These no-bake chocolate truffles make a great accompaniment to Saltaire's *Triple Chocoholic Stout*. If you don't want to venture too far into the 'Chocolate Zone', then you can always find a partner in Stouts, Porters and even Cherry Krieks or Black IPAs. Make a batch up, and get experimenting!

All you need to do is melt 4oz of plain cooking chocolate in a bowl over some steaming water. When melted, fold in 1½ oz of soft unsalted butter, 1oz of icing sugar, 1 tbsp. of double cream, and 1½oz of smashed up digestive biscuit crumbs.

Leave the mixture in the fridge for a little while to firm up, and then, using teaspoons and then your hands, roll into balls. Roll in chocolate vermicelli, and place back in the fridge to firm again. There you are – rich little chocolate truffles to satisfy any sweet tooth.

Summer Wine Brewery
Honley

It's a particularly perverse fact that some of the most experimental Ales in Yorkshire are being brewed with a brewery with a very traditional name. James Farran and Andy Baker, based in Honley, have a reputation for beers that are big in flavour and bite; owing more in influence to America than England. Traditional Yorkshire beer, by and large, this ain't. Or is it?

'It was simply a name we picked to give us a geographical location,' says James chuckling at the fact that they couldn't be further removed from the image of Compo and Clegg rolling down the green hills of Yorkshire in bathtubs. 'It gets people talking though! We've had drinkers from around the world tell us they've seen the show, so we get a lot of conversation out of it.'

That's not to say that Summer Wine Brewery distance themselves from the region – far from it. Recently rebranded, their slogan, 'Evolutionary Craft Beer from Yorkshire', confirms that, as well as introducing another key facet to the brewery's success: evolution.

'Some people have this impression of us that we only brew big, brash Ales,' says Andy. James continues: 'When you look at our range, we brew a Dark Mild at 3.7%, brewed with Northdown, Fuggles and Golding hops. We do monthly specials, too. But we are interested in all beer styles from across the globe – and show respect to that.'

The origins of the brewery can be traced back to 2006, where James learnt the ropes by homebrewing. This hands-on, self-taught schooling let James not only understand the nuts-and-bolts of brewing, but gave him the confidence that his beers were good. The feedback he was getting was amazing. 'I was in my cellar – registered with Customs – and was bottling my homebrew and selling it to Holmfirth Mills. I had a little stand in the shop, and I did quite well out of it. But it was a hobby, really.'

By 2008 that hobby was already threatening to outgrow his cellar when Andy Baker started working with him. Andy was biding his time before fulfilling an ambition of going to Canada on a kayaking trip, and decided to join James with his quest to take his brewing to the next level. It was time to get serious.

Only three months later, the lease was signed on their tiny brewery in Honley, near Holmfirth. Not long after that, the first Summer Wine brews began hitting the pubs of Yorkshire.

'In the early days, we were brewing traditional styles. We had a Yorkshire Bitter called *Vagabond*, *Holmfirth IPA* and a beer called *Furnace Gold*.' I point out how different those embryonic Summer Wine beers sound to their current range.

'In a rush to open the brewery, we hadn't really thought about it; the beers or the brand,' laughs James. Andy goes further: 'We were brewing beers that we thought the market wanted; a Bitter to compare to Black Sheep, for example. In reality, that market was crowded anyway. Plus, the beers were not really what we wanted to brew.'

In fact, James and Andy were spellbound by what was coming out of America: bittersweet, aggressively hopped beers that the likes of Stone, Dogfish Head and Rogue were producing. 'The first time I flipped the lid on a Stone IPA, I couldn't believe what I was smelling,' smiles James. 'It was like... *Wow*.'

Thus began Summer Wine's journey of expression with American hops, which – broadly speaking – produce a much more pronounced citrus and pine aroma than their English cousins. James continues: 'American hops just capture my

From left: Andy Baker, James Farran

senses in a unique way. We want to create that same experience: to amaze people when they smell our beers. We want them to crave more of it, and demand more of these kinds of beers.'

In 2010, the friends decided to test exactly how the beers in their head would be received in reality with Project Six: a series of six beers, all at 6% abv, single hopped with 6 different hops. As a concept, it was a success. The beers were not only tasty, fragrant and subtly aggressive in bite and strength, but the manner in which they were released – one at a time, once a month – made each arrival an event.

James reveals that Project Six was actually a dry-run for their now flagship beer: *Diablo IPA*. 'It was an experiment for us to see how these hops worked, and at the same time, we could see how these kinds of beers were received. It was market research, really.'

As James and Andy found their feet, more experimental beers began to emerge from sleepy Honley – an IPA hopped with seven hops, one sprinkled with malted rye and a Black IPA – only to receive the same rapturous approval. Summer Wine's new direction – big, flavoursome, hoppy beers – seemed to not only hit the spot with drinkers, but was distinguishing them from the rest of the pack. *Diablo*, the brewery's flagship IPA, became permanent and a marker for the "Summer Wine Style".

'*Diablo* is seen as a real Yorkshire IPA. It's won awards up and down the country and is in demand in Italy and Sweden now, but it's only been around for the last 18 months!' adds James, proud of the achievements of a beer that could have very easily disappeared without trace had it not been so refined and drinkable.

A rebrand followed; a new website and focus came along with it. Did eschewing more 'traditional' styles ever feel like a risk?' Both James and Andy emphatically state not. 'It's about the best beer that we can make. It's not about budget. What it costs, it costs, and we'll sell it accordingly.' Andy adds, '*Kopikat* (an Imperial Coffee-Vanilla Stout) was the most expensive beer we ever brewed, and it sold out immediately. We could have brewed *Kopikat* many times over.'

This is reflective of James and Andy's personality. Both are single-minded in whatever they do, whether it's unwinding by getting out in the country or indulging in a spot of philosophising about the more esoteric aspects of beer. The boys from Honley don't seem to do anything by half. When they began bottling in late 2011 – a notoriously laborious task – they did it themselves, on-site.

The brewery has also been slowly moving more of their beer from cask into keg. This might upset purists, but James asserts that the decision is purely based on flavour and giving their drinkers what they want.

'It was a natural progression for our beers, as they are American in style. With a full-bodied IPA, you want to give the beer a slight lift with a spritz of carbonation in there, just to clean the palate. As it happened, as we began to explore it, the market for keg beers was opening up. Landlords were selling out and asking for more, so we gave them it! We're happy to work like that. We brew cask Ales, but we brew for keg and bottle too. As simple as that.'

Evolutionary Craft Beer indeed, topped off with a typically Yorkshire attitude. James explains that both the slogan – and the location – is actually helping them establish themselves in new territories, acting as a reassurance of quality.

'Yorkshire beer isn't brown and boring. It's exciting and takes in all kinds of influences. In fact, we've had contact from all over the world, and are selling in Europe now. The fact that we are from Yorkshire is really a boost.'

So, what's the next stage of evolution for Summer Wine?

It would seem that success for the brewery lies beyond Yorkshire. A new brewery is planned, and the bottling operation is growing in strength monthly. The beers continue to remain popular across the UK, pointing to Summer Wine events in Edinburgh and London as proof of that. James and Andy are ensuring that the Yorkshire flag is being flown with pride.

James is unsure of what the future holds – but excited by the prospect. 'We're not going to rest on our laurels. We are going to brew more boundary-pushing, exciting beers than ever before, especially when we get the new brewery. That's the evolution of us, of Summer Wine.'

Whines and Spirits!

York's many glorious pubs claim to be haunted, with the Golden Fleece taking the crown as one of England's most haunted sites. Standing since at least 1503, the pub – which sits near York's famous Shambles – has reportedly been the home to at least ten different ghosts, one of which is a boy who was trampled to death by a drayman's horse. Gruesome!

PORTER

MALT PORTER

5.0%

S·B·W

DIABLO

IA PALE ALE

6.0%

ABV.

S·B·W

OHORT

DOUBLE BLACK BELGIAN
RYE PA

7.5% ABV.

Summer Wine Brewery

Crossley Mills, Honley, HD9 6QB

www.summerwinebrewery.co.uk

Diablo IPA Abv: 6%

As the name suggests, *Diablo* is a devil of a beer. A strong IPA with a rich, gold hue, *Diablo* is chock-full of robust character, overlaid with a pungent, powerful aroma of mango, strawberry, grapefruit and orange peel. The finish is typically sharp and risingly bitter, with plenty of warmth.

Try it with: Thai-spiced fish, mango chutney and spiced breads, hot cross buns

Teleporter Abv: 5%

Brewed with 10 different malts, *Teleporter* is supremely smooth, with creamy chocolate and Bourbon-biscuit notes in the body. The aroma is awash with smooth vanilla and milk chocolate, which continues into the taste. The finish is freshened up with liquorice and hints of blackcurrant. A fresher, more lively Porter than you'd maybe expect, but one that offers rich reward.

Try it with: duck confit with black cherry, Black Forest gateau, smoked bacon and beans

Rouge Hop Abv: 5%

Candy-apple red and superbly moreish, *Rouge Hop* has a nose full of grassy pine alongside some molasses and granary bread. Rich, full and sweet, that drying brown sugar note returns in the sip, where orange blossom and fresh grapefruit sidles up alongside lingering bitterness.

Try it with: spiced lamb chops, cheese-stuffed jalapeño peppers, crème caramel

Baked Feta

If you want to explore the potential of *Diablo IPA* as a great beer for food, try pairing it with baked feta.

The fruity, full-flavoured IPA complements perfectly the smooth, salty cheese, and the brisk, bitter finish of the beer is incredibly refreshing.

All you need to do is make a little foil parcel and lay a slab of good feta inside. Drizzle with a little good olive oil, and a sprinkle of mint and a few chilli flakes.

Bake in a hot oven until the top browns, and then serve to friends with a couple of bottles of *Diablo* and some warmed, sliced pitta bread for smearing that lovely feta onto.

Wharfebank Brewery
Nr Leeds

If there's one thing that Martin Kellaway does incredibly well, it's enthusiasm. The Southampton-born brewer radiates 'can-do' attitude and positivity – especially when it comes to his baby: Wharfebank Brewery.

In a previous life, Martin had pursued a career behind a different kind of wicket. Cricket was his love; dropping out of Exeter University for a professional contract at Hampshire Cricket Club. However, like many, many young men, Martin wasn't quite able make the grade as a sportsman. 'I simply knew that the guy in the first team was better than me!' he laughs, citing that early realisation as the main reason that he eventually hung up his wicketkeeper's gloves and joined Bass in the early 90s.

Joining the Bass Management Programme in Birmingham gave Martin grounding in numerous areas of the drinks industry, and he paid his dues in kind. A job at Britvic Soft Drinks was the pinnacle of that period, and it was here that he developed a keen eye for marketing and – perhaps more importantly – the launch of new businesses.

Working with pubs led to a number of lasting, useful partnerships, and before long he found himself working for Fuller's (brewers of iconic beers such as *London Pride* and *Chiswick Bitter* amongst others), looking after their bottled off-trade. 'Actually, I'm not a brewer by trade, if you think about it', he laughs, that disarming honesty bubbling to the fore again.

Switching from one well-known brand to another, Kellaway spent time working with Scottish giants Caledonian, specifically on the launch of their famous bottled IPA, *Deuchars*, in the UK. The final act in this period of his life, however, came when Heineken bought Caledonian. It was time, realised Martin, to do something new. He wanted not only to sell the beer, but make it. After a period travelling up and down the country, there was only one region that he wanted to make home. 'My vision was Wharfebank, and it had to be Yorkshire, really.'

He settled in the region, and, after a protracted financing period, he eventually secured money to start up the brewery – with a business partner in Nigel Jowett.

It wasn't all plain sailing, however. As stated before, Martin was not a qualified brewer. Dipping into that extensive black book of his, he realised he had the perfect man on hand to help him get Wharfebank's beers out of his head and into the pint glass.

He had become friends with Ian Smith – an ex-brewer at Tetley's – through the years and Ian jumped at the chance to work with Martin on the blueprints of the beer range. 'Ian and I created the beers initially. Ian knew what styles I was looking for, but he brought them to life. I wasn't a brewer, but I really knew what I wanted.'

This period of testing, tasting, tweaking and re-brewing was realised during 2008 at The Fox and Newt pub in Burley, Leeds. The Fox and Newt has enjoyed a long tradition of brewing on-site. The cellar holds a 3-barrel brewplant shoehorned (in a somewhat Heath Robinson fashion) within its whitewashed brick walls. Martin attacked the challenge with typical gusto, going the whole hog and running the pub as well.

'I took on the tenancy on a short-term basis,' he says. 'I wanted to cut costs so I ran the pub, lived there, and we trialled and tested the beers on the bar.'

Martin looks back at this period with fondness. It's clear that he found the creative aspect of brewing rewarding. 'We were calling ourselves "The Fox Brewing Company" – and we got things right about 80% of the time,' he chuckles.

Martin Kellaway (Photo courtesy of Wharfebank Brewery)

One beer in particular was received well by the thirsty punters of The Fox and Newt: a full-bodied, ruddy-hued Ale called *Fox Red*. Drinking in the pub at the time, I recall being impressed by a deeply smoked, nutty Dark Mild called *Clarendon*. The beers were good; no doubt about it; robust in flavour and a notch above the usual 'brewpub' fare.

Ian also provided the perfect foil to Martin: providing perspective from the other side of the bar. This venture wasn't just Martin's plaything; it was duty-bound to provide a complete drinking experience, something which Martin would occasionally lose sight of. 'At the end of the day, Ian made me realise that we had to provide a range, not just the beers that I wanted to drink. We've got to provide for everyone and we've got to be aware of what's going on elsewhere,' says Martin, clearly grateful to his friend's input and – at times – reality checks.

In 2010, with an armful of tried-and-tested beers under his arm, it was time for Martin to move on and make his dream a reality. Moving into a converted paper mill in Pool (just near Otley, on the outskirts of Leeds), Wharfebank Brewery was born: new brewery kit, a new team, and a new, modern image. The site turned out to be perfect – functional and picturesque.

'I wanted to be here; near Leeds but also rural, too. We're near Otley, Skipton and Ilkley, and that was the area we wanted to be in. We wanted to be a breath of fresh air, despite our outwardly traditional image.'

Martin and his team immersed themselves in their beer range. *Fox Red* became *CamFell Flame*, a robust Red Ale with a heavy hit of slightly smoky sweetness courtesy of an addition of demerara sugar. The brightly refreshing *Tether Blonde* and slightly maltier *Slingers Gold* soon followed. This trio of typically unfussy, easy-to-drink Ales provided a firm base for Wharfebank to muscle in on barspace across Yorkshire. They've since been joined by *VPA*: a citrus-led Pale Ale named after Verbeia, a goddess that, in Roman times, was the personification of the River Wharfe.

Despite the initial trepidation that many new brewers experience in picking up the phone and making those vital first sales calls, Martin reveals that Wharfebank were received well from the outset. 'We got into – and still are – in the good houses; places that I've drunk in for years,' states Martin, clearly proud at the network of publicans across Yorkshire serving great beer to eager customers on a daily basis. 'We're in Foley's and the Grove in Leeds, we're in the Star in Huddersfield,' he smiles, reeling off great pub after great pub. 'We're where I wanted Wharfebank to be. The support (from publicans) has been wonderful.'

The locals seem to have a specific taste for *Slingers Gold*, with the beer proving to be a massive hit in the cricket and rugby clubs across the region. 'Otley Rugby Club just loves it. They get through gallons of it!' laughs Martin, the ex-

(Photo courtesy of Wharfebank Brewery)

(Photo courtesy of Wharfebank Brewery)

sportsman in him clearly pleased at the prospect of many a game being dissected and debated in the clubhouse over tawny pints of frothy, restorative *Slingers Gold*.

There's also The Fleece, Wharfebank's pub, perching on the riverbank just outside Otley. Opened in 2011, The Fleece is a welcoming, typically no-nonsense pub where both the drinker and the diner are welcome. The menu itself is a treasure trove of locally-sourced produce that collides with Wharfebank's beers on the bar, from Yorkshire bangers and mash to a fish cocktail brimming with fresh, creamy Whitby crab.

'All of our food comes from Yorkshire where possible; freshly prepared and served alongside great beer. We call it Yorkshire grazing,' smiles Martin. The Fleece joins the likes of the Old Cock and the Horse and Farrier as focal points for visitors to Otley in search of quality Ales and good food.

The Fleece is doing well, and in early 2012 Wharfebank acquired another local pub, the Half Moon in Pool – literally on the brewery's doorstep. Local MP Greg Mulholland, who not only officially opened Wharfebank but considers them his local brewery, couldn't be happier at Wharfebank's commitment to the area.

'It was great news for the local pub scene when Wharfebank took on the Fleece – and now the Half Moon in Pool. They have not only saved and regenerated a fantastic historic Otley pub, but rejuvenated the village local in Pool, which is wonderful for both communities,' says Greg.

Still, Martin would like to get Wharfebank's beer a little further afield, and Wharfebank's beers will appear in bottles by the end of 2012. 'I think *CamFell Flame* would be great in a bottle; it'd be great on the dinner table,' enthuses Martin.

'People are crying out for our beers in bottles but it's got to be the right market,' he adds, cautiously, pointing out that Yorkshire would have to be the first and core market. Beer miles can often be the enemy of fresh, bottled beer.

Martin signs off our chat with a mantra that I have no doubt he embodies: hard work, laughter and graft. 'Everyone that works for us here has passion for beer, and we have a good little business here. However, we try and have a little fun along the way.'

Some would say that's a typically Yorkshire way of doing things.

(Photo courtesy of Wharfebank Brewery)

(Photo courtesy of Wharfebank Brewery)

Wharfebank Brewery

Pool Business Park, Pool in Wharfedale, LS21 1FD

www.wharfebankbrewery.co.uk

CamFell Flame Abv: 4.4%

The presence of demerara sugar in the brewing process gives *CamFell Flame* a heart of smooth bonfire toffee and a slight hint of gingerbread-like spice. Smooth, sweet and warming, this ruby-hued Ale is a real autumnal treat; rich and rewarding without being too heavy.

Try it with: treacle tart, chargrilled steak, lamb hotpot

Tether Blonde Abv: 4.1%

This Blonde has a light, fresh body which carries a subtle, honeyed note that starts smooth and then turns progressively drier as it finishes, which it does with suitably lemon-led flourish. A wonderfully refreshing beer that's incredibly easy to drink.

Try it with: grilled halloumi cheese with roasted red peppers, onion bhaji, game terrine

Slingers Gold Abv: 3.9%

A traditional, robustly satisfying Best Bitter. Light amber in colour, with a pleasantly sweet, floral aroma. There's digestive biscuit in the body and a slightly tart, crisp finish which invites the next sip.

Try it with: mustard-glazed ham, fish and chips, pork pie with pickles

Maple Biscuits

If you have a sweet tooth, these little biscuits are so easy to make and are a nice little accompaniment to a nutty, smooth pint such as *Slingers Gold*.

All you need to do is roll out a sheet of ready-made shortcrust pastry, and drizzle a little honey onto it. Shake cinnamon over that, evenly, and a few chopped almonds. Roll it up tightly, and then chill for 30 minutes in the fridge.

Slice it into rounds, and place onto a baking tray oiled with a little butter. Brush maple syrup onto the face of each one, and a few sprinkles of brown sugar. Pop into a pre-heated oven at 175°C for 25 minutes or so, glazing every ten. Cool, and enjoy!

Wold Top Brewery
Hunmanby

As we drive up the North Yorkshire Wolds towards the Mellor Farm, home of Wold Top Brewery, Gill Mellor points to the exact spot where their land begins: wild meadow, a crag of grey rock capping it, and almost 360° of verdant Yorkshire countryside surround it. Hares and pheasants leap out of the hedgerows as we pass, which at intervals give way to brilliant slashes of buttercup-yellow oilseed rape. In the balmy early-summer sunshine and endless blue sky, it's hard not to be impressed at the sheer splendour of it all.

Wold Top Brewery sits on the Mellors' 600-acre working farm that harvests wheat, barley and oilseed rape. It's large, but almost entirely self-sufficient. There aren't many breweries in the region that use their own barley, draw their own water from a borehole and generate their own electricity – even the kettle in the brewhouse is fired using gas. But make no mistake, this is no antiquated operation in a farmer's shed. Wold Top is a full-time brewery, replete with bar, bottling operation and fields for campers to enjoy one of the many events that they hold there year on year. As far as workplaces go, it's certainly one of the most picturesque.

The Wold Top story begins when Tom and Gill met at Wye University – well known for its development of UK hops such as Northdown, Bramling Cross and Challenger. Tom was studying agriculture, and Gill horticulture. After studies, the pair returned to the Mellor family farm, where life was becoming far from idyllic. 'In the late nineties, farm incomes were really plummeting,' recalls Gill. 'People were finding extra money by doing things like going into Bed and Breakfasting, but we didn't really fancy that.'

After a period of reflection, it occurred to them that the answer was – literally – right under their noses. 'East

Tom & Gill Mellor

Yorkshire is one of Europe's prime malting areas. There have been maltsters in this area for decades. The soil is ideal here, and we have our own water supply, which produces wonderfully pure, clean-tasting water.'

Tom's restless mind and eagerness to accept challenges put those two together, threw in a little knowledge of hops left over from his time from Wye, and cultivated his kernel of an idea.

The Mellors realised that brewing was a real possibility and began work on the beers and brewery with local brewery consultant David Smith. Family friends Derek and Katrina Gray – another farming family – liked the idea too, and offered to take part in the new venture.

'Our first beer was brewed in May 2003 – *Falling Stone*,' Gill recalls. The beer – named after a meteorite that infamously hit Derek's Wold Newton farm in 1795 – proved a local success. *Wold Top Bitter* followed shortly thereafter. Both are still in the stable of core beers produced at Wold Top. '*Wold Top Bitter* is still my favourite,' states Tom. 'I enjoy all of them, but always come back to the Bitter for it's clean, crisp flavour.'

As things tend to do when the beer is good, matters soon got out of hand. The little brewery was capturing people's imagination, and it soon became apparent that there would have to be a shift of focus.

'Within a month of our first brew I realised that it would become a full-time job,' says Tom. 'We were extremely happy with the response to our beer and realised the huge potential waiting to be tapped. I was so proud of the brewery and our beer.'

The brewery was only supplying locally at this stage – in pubs in places such as Scarborough and Bridlington – but Derek and Katrina decided that they needed to concentrate on farming and their own pub: the highly-regarded Falling Stone in Thwing.

So, in 2005, the Mellors took sole ownership of Wold Top. Since then, the brewery has expanded, with strong bottle sales being the catalyst to that growth. The move into bottling simply filled a necessity initially, but it became apparent very soon that having the space and ability to bottle your own beer was a useful ace up your sleeve.

'It got to the point where we just couldn't get our beer bottled fast enough at other contract brewers, so bottling our beer from early on really suited us. We didn't want to chase casks around the country. For us, the bottling line has been a really good investment.'

'We'd never lose cask beer, but we'd like to make our cask beer a little closer to us here, and get our bottles out a little further,' Gill continues, explaining her idea of the importance of the locality of beer. 'We're not an industrial unit in the middle of nowhere, we really do have skylarks and curlews

WOLD TOP
SCARBOROUGH
FAIR IPA

India Pale Ale

WOLDTOP
YORKSHIRE

Wold Famous
Golden
Summer

ENGLISH SUMMER

BREWED ON OUR

NATURALLY
The Wold Top Brewery
high on the hillside
way to the sea. We
brewed using softer
and our own spr
produce at our
INGREDIENTS:
Hops and Yeas
Gluten conten
than 700m

Wold Famous
WOLD
GOLD

Blonde Beer

WOLDTOP
YORKSHIRE

500ml 4.8% ABV.

AINST
THE
GRAIN

*ally
Free
e Ale*

Wold Famous

WOLD TOP
BREWERY

4.5% ABV
300ML

ten Free

Angler
REWA

*A Truly Relax
English Summer
fect for enjoying
Summers Afternoo*

WOLD TOP
BREWERY

5

SH SUMMER BE

here, we have our own ingredients. When someone drinks a pint of Wold Top, this,' she smiles, gesturing at our surroundings, 'is what you are drinking.'

Wold Top's beers consist of a core range of *Wold Gold*, *Wold Top Bitter*, *Headland Red* and *Angler's Reward*, and is supplemented by twelve seasonal specials, from a sprightly *Summer Ale* to winter's complex *Shepherd's Watch*. The beers are brimming with flavour and personality, and sell out quickly wherever they appear. Recent success has belonged to a new addition to the family: a little upstart by the name of *Against the Grain*.

A gluten-free beer, *Against the Grain* has something of a cult following in Yorkshire. Gluten-free beers are a difficult beast to get right; the lack of body often making for a disappointing drinking experience. Not so *Against the Grain* – it sings with bold, zingy flavour and is a firm warm-weather favourite in my household. What started out life as a contract brew for another party became an important part of the family.

'It was selling so well, and the people we were brewing it for weren't really pushing it, so we took it and tweaked the recipe to something that we were happy with,' smiles Gill, proudly.

It is certified gluten-free, but bridges a unique gap between people who have to drink gluten-free beer and those that choose to. 'We don't really advertise it as a 'GF-Free' beer. It stands on its own, and we have a number of pubs who demand it as soon as it's available. It's so popular!' laughs Gill. She need not sound so incredulous – it's a great beer. Recently, *Scarborough Fair IPA* (named as a tribute to the town's maritime history) has joined *AGG* – a powerful, marmalade-hued IPA in the classic British style – but brewed gluten-free.

Alongside Tom and Gill, brewing is looked after by Alex Balchin, with his team of brewers working on Wold Top's beers old and new. He finds working at Wold Top entirely a

From left: Kate Mellor, Alex Balchin, Gill Mellor

team effort. When discussing recipe formulation, he says: 'It's very organic. We just take ideas – based on a great beer we've enjoyed on an evening, perhaps – and work on them from there.' It's a cycle of tasting, testing and tweaking. He recalls a marathon tasting session of IPAs from around the world in order to decide where they wanted *Scarborough Fair* to sit in terms of flavour.

Gill also reveals that her taste in beer actually hails from another famous beer-producing region; one that produces beers with bold, brassy character in abundance due to its long history of hop-growing. 'When Tom and I were drinking beer in Kent in the seventies, we really enjoyed the local beer's full-bodied, hoppy nature. *Wold Top Bitter* is our tribute to that – it's a little sharper than you'd expect in Yorkshire. We've been really pleased with it.'

The brewery remains very much a family affair. Their daughter, Kate, helps out with accounts and bottling (in fact, a bit of everything!) and remains a font of knowledge for all things Wold Top. They've had more or less the same staff since their start, and work together as a family, rather than a business.

Wold Top's beers are starting to trickle into Europe, too. Gill talks with excitement about a connection that they've recently made in northern Italy, and there are enquiries coming in from Sweden, Canada, Norway and the United States. If things keep rolling as they are, it looks like people from further afield will be able to sample Wold Top's little corner of Yorkshire.

Beer Festivals

Beer Festivals are held throughout Yorkshire on an almost monthly basis – from ones organised by CAMRA to showcase the best of what the region has to offer, to independent festivals held to raise support for good causes, to ones that form part of larger food festivals. Get online and look up what's happening in your area; Beer Festivals are a great way to sample beers from a wide array of Yorkshire's brewers in one day.

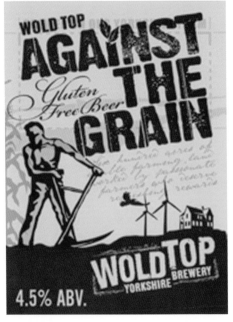

Wold Top Brewery

Hunmanby Grange, Wold Newton, YO25 3HS

www.woldtopbrewery.co.uk

Against The Grain Abv: 4.5%

Pale, pale gold in colour, *Against the Grain*'s aroma is packed with lemon and lime sherbet. The body is super-light, with some yeasty, freshly-baked bread notes, and the finish is vibrant, refreshing, and bursting with more lime pith. Fantastic on a warm day, slightly chilled.

Try it with: pork schnitzel, chicken and preserved lemon, feta and spinach tart

Headland Red Abv: 4.3%

Headland Red pours deep mahogany and boasts a tight, tan head. Full in flavour, there's mellow plum and cherry-skin in the body alongside hints of gingerbread and cereal, and the finish is short, snappy and crisp. An incredibly rewarding beer with plenty of character.

Try it with: beef casserole, lamb tagine, pain au raisin

Wold Gold Abv: 4.8%

Incredibly versatile, award-winning Golden Ale from the Wold Top crew. Straw in colour with a sunny disposition, *Wold Gold* carries smooth, creamy oat flavours in the body and wraps everything up in an earthy, softly fruity finish with a hint of peach.

Try it with: Welsh rarebit, tomato and red pepper chutney, honey-glazed pork chops

Kofta

If it's a Greek-inspired meal you fancy, kofta are so simple to make. Mix a 50/50 blend of lamb and pork mince with fresh mint, oregano, salt and black pepper, and leave it to sit overnight, covered, in the fridge.

When it's time to eat, take a handful of the mince and roll into balls - about the size of a golf ball. Brown them in a large pan in a little oil, then finish off in a hot oven until cooked through. Serve with a Greek salad of tomato, olives, cucumber, feta cheese, and flatbreads. Don't forget the tzatziki! Enjoy with a bottle of fridge-cold *Against The Grain*.

ALBION
BREWERY
LEEDS LTD
FINE ALES &
STOUT
On Draught & In Bottle

Beer in the Kitchen

'Beer and Food Matching' has become a popular term in recent years, popping up on menus and as the theme of events all over the country. In reality, pubs, restaurants and bars are latching on to what many of us have known as a matter of course: beer tastes great with food – food tastes great with beer.

We have some of the best produce in the country in Yorkshire, and it would be a crime not to enjoy it with beer from our region. Over the next few pages, I've put together some recipes for you to try, or even simply use as a jumping-off point for your own experimentation.

Beer and food doesn't have to be complex. Think of a ploughman's platter with a tart IPA, or a fresh, hot pork pie with a glowing, amber pint of Best. So if you're still not sure, *just try it*. Bring beer into your kitchen. I guarantee you won't regret it.

Blue Cheese and Smoked Bacon Risotto

Risotto couldn't be easier to make; a simple, comforting supper that can pack a massive hit of flavour. You can flavour risotto any way you like, but if you like the strong, smoked notes in Stout, then this blue cheese and bacon variant is for you. The salt of the bacon and cheese is perfect for dark, rich beers like Stout. If you're a vegetarian, then simply leave out the bacon and use vegetable stock.

(Feeds two generously)

You will need:

250g risotto rice

1 pt stock (chicken)

4 rashers good smoked bacon (preferably from Yorkshire!)

blue cheese

butter

olive oil

black pepper

chopped rosemary to taste

1. First, you'll need to get your rice cooking. Gently melt a knob of butter in a large pan or stockpot with a dash of olive oil. Add the rice, and stir to ensure all the grains are coated.

2. Add your stock – slowly – and simmer the rice on a gentle heat. The rice will soak up the stock and each time this happens, add some more. Keep stirring to avoid burning.

3. In the meantime, sauté your bacon in a pan. You want it crispy, but not burned. When the bacon takes on colour, add the chopped rosemary to the oil to simply add a hint of flavour in the meat. Remove from the heat once cooked.

4. After 20-25 minutes or so, your rice will be cooked.

5. Now, you can add your blue cheese to the rice. Chop it into blocks, and crumble in. If you vary the size of the chunks, some will melt and coat the rice; others will remain whole for you to find within the risotto. Finally, add a twist of black pepper.

6. Serve immediately, with the bacon on top. Pour your Stout and enjoy!

Braised Red Cabbage
& Sausages

Braising red cabbage is my favourite way to cook it; you can leave it in the oven and get on with other things. It's a tasty accompaniment to chicken, pork – or in this case, really good sausages. Not only that, but it also makes a surprisingly light alternative to Sunday lunch. A simple, nutty Bitter, ESB or Brown Ale perfectly complements this dish; and feel free to add a dash of beer to the braising liquid, too.

(Feeds four as a side dish, two as a main)

You will need:

1 medium-sized head of red cabbage

pork bones, bacon or ham pieces

good quality sausages – 3 per person

½ pt chicken stock

ESB, Bitter or Brown Ale

large knob unsalted butter

2 tsp caster sugar

star anise

cinnamon stick

white pepper

salt

1. Pre-heat your oven to 160°C, and chop your cabbage into strips.

2. In a large casserole dish that can take direct heat, melt the butter and then add the cabbage, turning to coat in the butter. Dust with the sugar, white pepper (a couple of pinches) and a little salt, and turn again. Add the pork (bones, ham or bacon), and finally your star anise and cinnamon stick.

3. Stir well, cover with stock and a drop of your beer.

4. On a direct flame, bring to the boil.

5. Place a lid on the casserole dish and transfer to the oven and braise for at least two hours at 150°C. It's ready when the stock is absorbed.

6. Cook your sausages as normal, and serve on top of the cabbage.

Chicken in Brown Ale

I got the idea for this after daydreaming about a favourite dish of mine – stifado: the Greek rabbit stew with red wine, vinegar and onions. Using beer gives this dish an almost Belgian personality, with the most tender, braised chicken you'll ever taste! Also, try and track down smoked garlic – it really adds a depth of flavour. Serve with the beer you've used – you'll get a great result with stronger, darker Ale such as Cropton's *Monkman's Slaughter* – and crusty, fresh brown bread. A Barley wine would also suffice if you wanted a more pronounced beer flavour.

(Feeds Two)

You will need:

1 whole chicken, quartered

1 head smoked garlic, crushed

20 shallots, peeled

strong Brown Ale

1 tin chopped tomatoes

4 fresh tomatoes

fresh oregano

malt vinegar

brown sugar

olive oil

black pepper

salt

1. Take your chicken and, in a large stockpot, brown all over on a high heat in olive oil. Don't overcook them; you just want to brown the skin. When at that stage, remove to a plate, leaving the oil in the pan.

2. Drop your peeled shallots into the oil and brown. Leave them whole, and don't be afraid to let them catch a little and caramelise. This will just add another sticky-sweet aspect to the flavour.

3. Add about ¾ pt of beer to your shallots, and bring that to a gentle simmer. Season with salt, black pepper, and your sugar. (Feel free to drink the remaining beer as you go – cook's bonus!)

4. Add your tinned tomatoes, chopped fresh tomatoes, a little water, a hearty splash of malt vinegar, and your oregano.

5. Finally, add your garlic – all of it – and stir well.

6. Leave to simmer for about 90 minutes on a low heat. You just want to reduce the sauce with a gentle rolling bubble. Don't let it go dry – if you think it will, then it's too high. Give it a gentle stir every half hour or so.

7. Serve with bread and your beer. If the sauce needs thickening, do so with a little cornflour mixed with cold water.

Easy Beef Satay

Beef satay isn't something you see a lot of; it's usually chicken or pork. Peanut, garlic and chillies are a wonderful partner for beef, and the addition of soy sauce gives the whole dish a deep, comforting flavour. Also, as long as you marinate the beef ahead of time, it's a really easy dish to make. Beer-wise, you could go for a sweet, full-bodied beer such as Ossett's *Big Red* or Copper Dragon's *Challenger IPA*.

(Feeds Two)

You will need:

2 good quality rump steaks

1 head of pak choi

1 bunch spring onions

2 large mushrooms, washed

200g salted peanuts

sesame or peanut oil

soy sauce

For the marinade: 3 cloves garlic (chopped), chopped fresh ginger (1 inch), 1 whole chilli (deseeded & chopped), dark soy sauce, dash of oyster sauce, pinch of Chinese five-spice powder, dash of sesame or peanut oil, salt and black pepper

1. With a sharp knife, slice your beef into strips, as thinly as you can. Transfer to a large mixing bowl.

2. Add all the marinade to the beef, and then stir well to coat all the meat. Double-wrap with cling film, and marinate in the fridge at least overnight.

3. When you are ready to eat, slice your mushrooms, pak choi and spring onions, leaving some of the spring onions aside for garnish.

4. In a large pan, heat a spoonful of sesame or peanut oil, and lightly sauté the pak choi. Add a spoonful of boiling water, to create a little steam. After a short while, the pak choi will start to wilt. At this stage, add your mushrooms and spring onions, adding a little more oil and a splash of soy sauce. This will create a little liquid, with which you use to lightly braise the pak choi, spring onions and mushrooms in, on a high heat.

5. Finally, stir-fry your beef in a hot wok for just a couple of minutes. Keep it moving, and when cooked, plate up.

6. Garnish with the peanuts and spring onions, and serve with the cooked spring onions, pak choi and mushrooms.

Goats' Cheese Crostini with Pineapple and Jalapeño Salsa

The only thing you have to cook with this recipe is the salsa – the goats' cheese and bread you can buy as you wish. As usual, buying the best, locally produced cheese and bread will give you the tastiest results. You can make the salsa as hot as you like. My suggestion is for a zingy, sweetly piquant heat. I've paired this specifically with Magic Rock's *Cannonball IPA* here, but if you can't find that then opt for any IPA – you want a good level of citric bitterness to contrast with the salsa and bite of the cheese.

(Makes one. Just multiply as you see fit)

You will need:

good quality goats' cheese, sliced into rounds

ciabatta, sliced

1 tin pineapple chunks

20g jalapeño slices, chopped (use ones from a jar, not fresh)

1 tbsp marmalade

1. Firstly, you need to make your salsa. Drain the pineapple chunks but reserve the liquid. Pour the chunks into a saucepan and gently simmer, mashing the fruit a little with your spoon until it starts to break down.

2. When this happens, add the marmalade, and the reserved pineapple juice. Simmer again until reduced and a little jammy – about 15 minutes on a low heat.

3. Add your jalapeños, along with a splash of the vinegar from the jar.

4. Keep gently simmering and stirring until the salsa reaches a gummy, jammy consistency that you're happy with.

5. Meanwhile, slice your ciabatta, brush with a little olive oil and toast under a hot grill.

6. Place your goats' cheese on top. At this point, you can return the cheese to the grill for colour.

7. Top with the salsa, pour your beer and enjoy!

Pork & Apple Pinwheels

My grandfather was a butcher and my brothers and I used to help out in his shop on weekends. We'd make these little pastry morsels with my uncle, and they'd sell well for barbecues and outdoor parties. They make an ideal sweet/savoury snack for when the weather's warm. Crisp, refreshingly fruity Pale Ales will make an absolute treat of a partner. You can make your pastry, but I find ready-made is perfectly fine if you don't have the time. You could also make these and freeze them too – providing your meat and pastry is fresh.

(Makes two foot-long rolls, enough for about 4 people)

You will need:

1½lbs minced pork

1 carrot, finely chopped

1 red onion, finely chopped

4 spring onions, chopped

1 chilli, deseeded and chopped

300g flaky pastry

1 large, firm-fleshed apple, finely chopped

1 beaten egg, to glaze

olive oil

seasoning: salt, white pepper, fresh thyme, sage and parsley

1. In a large bowl, mix the pork with the chopped carrot, red onion, spring onions, chilli, apple and the herbs. Season with a little salt and white pepper.

2. Roll out your pastry, and lay flat on a floured surface. With your hands, spread the mixture across the pastry, leaving a gap of about half an inch at the edges.

3. Very carefully, roll the pastry up tightly – like a meaty Swiss roll. If it's too loose and it will not hold together, you'll have a big pinwheel log at this stage.

4. Repeat with as much pastry and meat as you have.

5. Place in the fridge to firm up and chill for at least an hour.

6. When ready to cook, simply slice with a very, very sharp knife (not a serrated one) into portions and arrange on a baking tray. The knife must be sharp and you must use a smooth action – or the pastry will tear.

7. When on the greased tray, you can apply a little beaten egg to the sides of the pastry, and brush a swirl of olive oil on the face of each one.

8. Bake in a preheated oven at 180°C for about 30 minutes, or until golden.

Porter Cake

This recipe was one of the most popular posts of all-time on my blog – and people are still asking for it! There's something about the alchemy that happens when dark, rich beer and fruit cake meet that makes it such a classic pairing: sweet and spicy, rich and robust. Originally, I used an American Porter, but you can use any you can find. If Porter isn't available (it's not a massively prolific style) then Stout would be good. Acorn's *Old Moor Porter* and Elland's *1872 Porter* are particularly fine.

As with most fruit cakes, it improves in flavour if you leave it for a few days in an airtight container before eating.

You will need:

175g of butter

400g mixed dried fruit

juice of one whole orange (along with grated zest)

175g muscovado sugar

½ bottle Porter or Stout

1 tsp bicarbonate of soda

300g plain flour

50g chopped nuts (hazelnuts, pecans or walnuts – or all three!)

1 tsp cinnamon

1. In a large pan, while stirring, melt the butter and sugar, and bring to the boil. Simmer for 15 minutes, stirring often to get that sugar dissolved. Add the beer, orange juice and peel.

2. After 15 minutes or so, allow it to cool for ten minutes and add the dried fruit. Then, stir in the bicarbonate of soda. Note: it will foam up at this point, but don't worry – this is what's supposed to happen. Just keep stirring and it will die down.

3. In a large bowl, mix together the plain flour, chopped nuts and the cinnamon.

4. Once cooled, pour your wet mixture into the dry mixture and stir well. Finally, add 3 beaten eggs and stir thoroughly.

5. Heat your oven to 150°C and line and grease your baking or loaf tin. Pour the mixture into the tin and sprinkle more muscovado sugar on top. When the oven is ready, cook for about 90 minutes – checking after an hour or so by pricking with a skewer. If it comes out clean from the middle, then it's done.

6. Once cooled, enjoy a slice with the rest of your Porter, or leave in an airtight container for a week before enjoying.

Rosemary Lamb Chops
with Black Pudding Couscous

Although you normally think of pork when you think of black pudding, its deep, lightly spiced character works perfectly with lamb, too. You can use it in a stuffing, or – as I have done here – simply make an interesting, light couscous to partner herby, sweet lamb chops. To accompany, pick a robust, sweet Ale – don't go for hoppy beers. Copper Dragon's *Scotts 1816* or Haworth Steam Brewery's *Ironclad 957* would be perfect. It's a light, herby alternative to a traditional Sunday roast.

(Feeds two)

You will need:

3 lamb cutlets per person

200g couscous

2 slices good quality black pudding, cubed (I used Lishman's)

1 roasted red pepper, chopped (marinated, from a jar)

olive oil

fresh rosemary

fresh mint

salt

black pepper

1. About an hour before cooking, place a sprig of rosemary on each of your cutlets, and cover in cling film. This will just help a little of the rosemary to permeate the meat.

2. When you are ready to cook, place the cutlets under a hot grill. Turn occasionally, but keep an eye on them – they'll take about 20 minutes or so. Don't let them burn!

3. Whilst the lamb is cooking, prepare your couscous by putting it in a pan and just covering it with boiling water. Put a lid on it, and leave it alone.

4. In a large pan, pour in a little olive oil, sauté your cubes of black pudding until crisp on all sides. Add your chopped pepper and stir together.

5. When the couscous is cooked, sprinkle your mint through it and then add it to the pan. Coat the grains in the oil from the pan, and gently mix with the black pudding and pepper.

6. All you need to do now is arrange your lamb with the couscous, pour your beer and enjoy your meal!

Acknowledgements

Many people helped me make this book happen. First and foremost, I'd like to thank all the brewers involved. Not only did you give up your time to speak to me at length about your work, but your honesty and warm welcome - not to mention your support for this project - was vital in ways you can't imagine. This is your story, and one that I am proud to tell.

I'd also like to thank all at Great Northern and David Joy for having faith in the book from the start; and David Burrill and Ross Jamieson for shaping my ramblings into the book you hold in your hands. Greg, thanks for your continuing hard work for our region and breweries, and for supporting the book so wholeheartedly.

Finally, Louise. Thank you. Without your unconditional support this book simply would not exist.

Leigh